A Smack at the Boche

The World War 2 diary and photographs of Leading
Seaman Ronald Turner aboard the British cruiser
HMS Hawkins 1939-1941

Johnny Parker

Contents

Uncle Ronnie Goes to War 1

1st September 1939 to 7th January 1940 3

9th to 27th January 1940 15

28th January 1940 27

29th January 1940 35

30th January to 9th February 1940 48

10th to 14th February 1940 57

15th to 29th Feb 1940 63

2nd to 5th Mar 1940 70

6th to 15th Mar 1940 75

16th Mar to 12th Apr 1940 81

18th Apr to 11th May 1940 92

12th May to 7th June 1940 103

9th Jun to 6th Sep 1940 109

12th Jan to 28th Sep 1941 134

We are going home - thank God 151

Reader List 155

To Uncle Ronnie

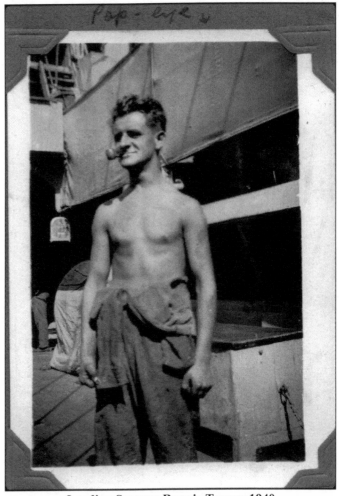

Leading Seaman Ronnie Turner 1940

Acknowledgements

I'd like to thank my brother Alistair and sister Margaret for sharing their memories of our Uncle Ronnie.

The diary text is an unedited transcription; there are no spelling or grammar corrections.

Join my Reader List

Join my reader list to get advanced notifications of new books and exclusive reader offers.

johnnyparker.uk/reader-list/

CHAPTER 1

Uncle Ronnie Goes to War

It's summer 1939 and Europe is a pan of milk coming to the boil heated by the furious expansionism of Hitler's Nazi Germany. National Service has been brought back and despite Neville Chamberlain's promise of 'peace in our time' everyone knows that war is inevitable.

Ronnie Turner, a south coast holiday camp sous chef, knew it. He had already joined the Royal Naval Volunteer Reserve (RNVR) and was no doubt licking his lips at the prospect of having "a smack at the Boche."

On Sunday 2nd September 1939 the radio announced to an expectant nation that a state of war existed between Britain and Germany. Ronnie had already quit his job on the Friday and travelled back to Liverpool to pack his bag for the fight.

Two weeks later armed only with his tattoos, an appetite for rum, a Box Brownie camera and an "illegal" small black notebook that would contain his thoughts and experiences for the next two years, Ronnie headed for Portsmouth and the most exciting period of his life.

South American steak was now on the menu instead of South Coast sausages. Ron would be swapping tattoo stories with the man who masterminded the first British victory of the war at the Battle of the River Plate, Admiral Harwood, as well as first hand accounts of the battle from a survivor and the Admiral himself.

There would be beer in Rio and tea from a pickle jar and German and Italian prisoners and rescuing shipwrecked sailors.

But there would also be times when he wished to back in his Liverpool bed when doused in the freezing South Atlantic waters for days on end.

The guns made him deaf, the sea froze him to the bone, Brazilian beer drank all his wages, the tropical sun fried his brain and long hours on watch drove him to distraction, but he never lost his desire to have a 'smack at the boche'. The question is, did he ever manage it?

CHAPTER 2

1st September 1939 to 7th January 1940

Bayonet Practice in the Navy

Ronnie arrived home eager to go to war, but his Mother and sisters were pretending everything was normal and heading off to North Wales for a late summer holiday.

Ronnie was one of seven kids with two older brothers and four sisters (my mother Josie is top left). His father, William, one of the pioneers of tattooing in Liverpool, had died just three years earlier. Billy 32, Alan 26 and Ron 24, the bachelor brothers, were all eligible for call up. Their mother Lillian (bottom left in above photo) must have worried she might lose all her sons and her income, a prospect facing countless mothers at the start of hostilities.

It only took two weeks for Ronnie's call up papers to arrive and he was off to Pompey for basic training. This consisted of a lot of drill and bizarrely, bayonet practice, not a skill you would think was needed in the Navy!

He wasn't alone, about 875,000 men joined up at the start of the war so it's not surprising that Ronnie had to sleep on a table when arriving at barracks and 'kick up a stink' to get his breakfast. The logistics of housing, feeding and clothing that many men would have been overwhelming.

While Ronnie was patrolling the Zoo, no doubt ensuring there was no monkey business, his future ship, HMS Hawkins, was being de-mothballed and re-armed ready for action, just like Ronnie.

Christmas 1939 saw Ronnie get a couple of days at home before joining HMS Hawkins and heading off to war. Despite the Portsmouth to Liverpool return fare being nearly a month's wages, Ronnie was desperate to see his Ma and sisters. It must have been an emotional Christmas with the prospect that it could well be the last they would spend together.

Ships were already being lost, three ships had already been sunk by mines before Ronnie had even set sail. But being a typical scouse pugilist, Ronnie wasn't put off and was itching for a fight. The next question was where would that fight be, frozen Russia or the South Atlantic to tackle the Graf Spee?

a smack @ the Boche

FRIDAY 1ST SEPTEMBER 1939 HAYLING ISLAND, HAVANT. WAR!

Friday 1st September 1939 Hayling Island, Havant. War! Everybody down here is talking about it. The whole holiday camp is seething with rumours. Germany has invaded Poland, the Chef has been called up, and the 2nd has gone home to take up his duties as Warden. I have refused to take over the Chef's job as the management has refused to higher my wages. I have also decided to go home as I'm a member of the RNVR and if war is declared I shall probably be called-up and I want to have a few days with my family.

Saturday 2nd September. Arrived home this morning 06:00 and found the girls are preparing for a weeks holiday in North Wales. Good luck to them. Reported to HMS Eaglet. Told to go home and wait for telegram.

Sunday 3rd September. War declared or should I say a state of war exists between England and Germany.

14th September. Received mobilisation papers. Shall have to report to HMS Eaglet with full kit etcetera. I've been waiting a fortnight for this.

16th September, Saturday. Reported to ships medical exam.

September 18th, Monday. Arrive Lime Street station 07:10. Join up with units. Catch 07:50 train for London. Arrive Euston, bus to Waterloo. Dinner Union Jack Club. Catch train for Portsmouth. Arrive Pompey and pile into lorry for Barracks and settle down. Received station card, allocated to C2 Mess. Find no bed vacant, sleep on table - drew loan bedding earlier on.

Tuesday 19th September. No Breakfast. Mess caterers excuse, not victualled for, kick up stink, get breakfast. First meal since dinner Monday. Draw belts, bayonets, gaiters and rifle sling. Marched to Victory Barracks and draw our gas mask, gas chamber test, etc.

September 30th we had drill on H.A. and A.A. guns (H.A. is High Angle and A.A. is Anti-Aircraft), small arms drill, bayonet practice, etcetera. Now have 16 days leave, glad to be home for a spell and have some hot grub. Now back at Excellent Barracks and in to the routine; 06:45 wakened, 07:55 fall in on Quarter Deck for cleaning quarters, 08:30 secure, 08:40 fall in in drill shed for divisions, 09:00 short service by chaplain, Roman Catholics have fallen out, 09:10 proceed to drill.

October 21st. I've not kept this diary up to date very much as one day is much like the another. It's becoming very monotonous. I've not much to report except for target towing and ammunitioning ships. Duty weekend for me this week, I have been given number 9 post to patrol during the day time I have to patrol the aviary and zoo. After sunset I join up with number 8 and patrol the office block. I've had this post about 4 times already, it's about time I had a change.

Monday November 6th. What a weekend, it rained non stop and my boots are like sieves. I'm due a long weekend and I'm taking it. The fare is stiff, 31 and 5 pence, but it's worth it. 16:00 Friday till first train Monday morning from Liverpool, that'll give me 2 full days at home. I think Ma and the girls will be glad to see me. Reckon we'll be drafted end of this month.

November 23rd. I've been unable to keep this diary up to date owing to having smashed my finger ammunitioning the Aurora. I start class on Monday 27th November to qualify for Quarters Rating 3rd Class. If I pass out I'll be entitled to a badge and threepence a day! Plenty of talk about the Gypsy being blown up by a mine outside Hawich harbour, the cruiser Belfast is also reported sunk and the Adventurer is supposed to have ad the guts blown out of her by a mine. Hoping to get Christmas leave, I've a little bloke down here for a mate, he's a tormenting rascal. I've got him to write to our Joan, they make a pair!

December 1st. We have been drafted to Pompey as Dockyard Defence and we move out of Whale Island and into RNB Victory. Christmas leave is still pretty sure. We have Lewis Gun posts scattered around the dockyard to man.

December 5th. 6 days leave. Draft leave! I've been drafted to HMS Hawkins in a hurry.

HMS Hawkins at Simonstown SA

December 11th. Arrived back at Royal Navy barracks, proceed to ship same day. First job, over the side to paint the ship!

December 19th. Sailed to test engines.

December 20th. At sea. Special sea duties, Telegraphsman on Lower Bridge. I am a Topsman. Ship is divided into three parts, Fo'csle, Top and Quarter Deck. Extra blankets issued, skipper thinks we are going to the North Atlantic. Our original cruise was to be South Atlantic with two six inch cruisers after Graf Spee.

December 24th Christmas Eve. We've put into port again. C in C pleased with condition of ship. Grants 48 hours leave to each watch.

December 25th Christmas Day. Change into Number One's and catch 12:40 train for home. Arrived about 07:30 big surprise.

December 26th. Quiet day at home. Caught midnight train for London, arrived 04:40, taxi to Waterloo, 05:27 train for Pompey, arrive 08:00 one hour adrift, taken before Officer of the Watch, on Commanders Report.

December 27th. Sailed for Portland, arrived evening, quiet trip closed up around gun. Sammy coats issued, great help in keeping warm.

January 6th 1940. We've been doing speed trials and sub-calibre and full calibre shoots
- good shooting, fired a tin fish too. But too hazy for AA (Anti-Aircraft) shoot.

Had an air raid warning and cleared for action but nothing happened, disappointed. Topees and canvas shoes issued last night. They seem to have changed their minds again and are sending us where it's warm.

Sunday Jan 7th. Back to Pompey for provisioning, fell in 07:10 to load the lighter, very fine drizzle. Finished loading and Commander issued those who draw Rum an extra tot. The skipper of the lighter also gave me two bottles of beer, which with the two tots of Rum has made me very happy - pipe down for the rest of the day.

P.1. 4" H.A. Gun at Practice

CHAPTER 3

9th to 27th January 1940

Atlantic or Arctic

After a great deal of square bashing and finger bashing, Ronnie was finally off to sea. At about this time the slogan 'careless talk costs lives' was born and perhaps the Captain had this in mind as the crew were kept in the dark about their destination until after leaving their first port of call in Freetown, Ivory Coast, and were safely in the middle of the South Atlantic.

Ronnie doesn't say too much about his ship but she was a fairly meaty piece of kit. HMS Hawkins was a heavy cruiser belonging to the Hawkins class of five cruisers. This new class of Cruiser had been designed in 1915 (coincidentally the same year that Ronnie was born) and named after Elizabethan sea captains.

Hawkins main armament was seven 7.5-inch guns plus eight 4-inch guns that could be used at a high angle to shoot at aircraft. Ronnie was a loader on one of the 4-inch guns, and the transition from loading sausages into a holiday camp frying pan to loading 12lb high explosive shells into a cannon seemed to have been a seamless one for Ronnie. He reflects on "the duties of the Navy" but thinks nothing of it. To him and his crewmates, protecting their country was all in a day's work.

As Hawkins put into Freetown on the Ivory Coast for supplies, he can only think of how lucky he is on watch in the middle of a January night, dressed in just his shorts, while the folks back home are shivering in the winter chill. He perhaps didn't realise that rationing had just been introduced and the folks back home were shivering at the thought of three rashers of bacon per week and one egg while he enjoyed more African oranges than he could poke a stick at. No scurvy here!

It's clear that thoughts of home were never far away and back in the day, a good old fashioned letter was the only way to keep in touch. News that a ship carrying mail had been sent to the bottom must have been a double blow to morale.

All the South American countries were neutral at this point in the war and continued trading with both the Allied and Axis sides. Hawkins task was to join the Navy's attempt to try and intercept 'blockade runners' and hunt down Merchant Raiders.

The blockade of Germany in the First World War was one of the principle reasons for their ultimate defeat. The British government, realised they would need to win the economic war a second time and immediately instigated a system to restrict the supply of raw materials to Germany.

The British Navy was vastly superior in numbers to Germany and used this advantage to restrict shipping from neutral ports that would have been carrying what it considered as 'contraband' for the enemy war effort.

Britain was able to control the flow of shipping going through the English Channel from the West and into the North Sea from Scandinavia. It also, with the aid of France (the fourth largest Navy at the time), controlled both ends of the Mediterranean, at Gibraltar and the Suez Canal.

Britain also had a massive intelligence network via its commercial contacts in every major port. Using tip-offs from bankers to stevedores, the British knew the contents of nearly every ship afloat. One of Hawkins' main duties therefore was to challenge shipping as to their identity and destination, forming a part of the greater intelligence network. If necessary they would be able to stop and detain any ship that was carrying contraband.

Ronnie mentions they were on a sharp lookout for German Merchant Raiders. These heavily armed merchant ships shadowed the shipping lanes looking for isolated ships to sink or capture. Like the U-Boats, they were part of Germany's stealth approach to the war at sea and very successful.

Carrying the fight to the enemy was Ronnie's principle aim. But if he couldn't find a German to batter he was more than happy to clobber anyone else who crossed him, even a senior rank. That makes him sound a bit of a monster but I knew him as a kind and generous soul who liked a pint and enjoyed a laugh. But, like his older brother Billy and his two younger sisters (my mum included), he was very quick tempered. I'm pretty sure he got this from his Irish father William Turner.

Before the war, William ran a tattoo and photographic studio at 44a Lime Street, now the site of the long closed down ABC Cinema (ironically bombed in the blitz). He had strong links with the boxing community and tattooed and photographed Ike Bradley the first Liverpool boxer to challenge for the world bantamweight title in 1911. I've no doubt Ronnie was influenced by his father's illustrious clients.

As a boy, Ronnie lived across the road from St George's Hall, one of the finest neo-classical buildings in Europe, but Liverpool, as well as being the second city of the Empire, was a rough port and he would have had to be street wise and handy with his fists to survive.

Ronnie was a classic British Bulldog, not afraid to have a go at anyone and if the Boche weren't available to smack, then his Acting Petty Officer had better beware.

TUESDAY JANUARY 9TH. SET SAIL. TORPEDO SHOOT

Tuesday January 9th. Set sail. Torpedo shoot, visibility bad. AA shoot cancelled. Continued to our destination, as yet unknown.

Jan 14th Sunday. To date we have been 5 days at sea. Freetown South Africa is to be our first port of call. We had a little swell crossing the Bay of Biscay. Quite a few of our lads were seasick. I was quite alright. We have had a few alarms during the night watches. It's rather a bore being closed up around the gun for 4 hours at a time. We are keeping watches at night since we sailed. We have discarded jerseys and jumpers and are running around in our slips. So far the weather has been delightful. I hope it keeps up. I have no idea where our final destination will be, South America, Bermuda, West Indies, who knows?

Monday Jan 16th. We have been issued with tropical rig, 2 shirts, 2 shorts, mine fit where they touch. Don rig. Nice and cool.

Ronnie in Tropical Rig

Tuesday 17th January. Arrived Freetown. The locals came out and dived for pennies. Exchanging fruit and baskets and plaited slippers for old clothes. I didn't bother bartering and bought what fruit I wanted at a canteen. By the end of the cruise baskets etcetera will be worse for wear. Wednesday - Finished

oiling and the Commander has made us work
both afternoons we were here and boy was
it hot. No shore leave allowed, sailed at
dusk.

Thursday Jan 18th. We are going to
the River Plate, Montivideo. Taking over
as Flagship from Achillies. I'm sorry we
are gettin Admiral aboard, more cleaning
and painting - no fun in this weather.
Saw my first shark.

Friday 19th January. Second
inoculation. It doesn't seem to affect me
like it does the others, my arm swells
but the pain goes quick. At dawn, while
closed up, we sighted a merchant ship.
She failed to answer signals, boarding
party ready. Closed up with live ammo.
Ship answered signals. An armed
merchantman is operating in these waters.
Hope we meet with her.

Saturday 20th Jan. Pay day. Crossed
the equator 02:00. Weather if anything is
cooler, am getting quite sunburned. I
forgot to mention, bought plenty of
oranges. Forty for a shilling. I'd give a
quid for a nice cool drink of Threlfalls
Wallop - I wonder how long I'll be out
here? These Whites are causing a lot of

dobying. Bought myself a bucket to wash in, two and six.

Sunday 21st. Divisions - excused as we have forenoon watch. Commander gave us a little speech, condition of ship etcetera. We have had no shore leave now since Christmas, Boxing Day to be precise. Harwood is the Admiral we are getting, still hot.

Mon 22nd Jan - at sea. Kept a keen lookout. German armed merchant cruiser reported in the vicinity. Carried eight 6 inch guns. Still very busy painting ship and titivating her up. According to Commander expect to be at least 100 days at sea without touching port and then we'll go into some quiet harbour for 5 days and rest. I don't think we'll be at sea that long. They are going to transfer some ratings to Achilles and some from Achilles to us. There are too many R.N.R and R.N.V.R and R.F.R ratings aboard and we're breaking their hearts. They tried to discipline us in the "good" old naval way, but they've given it up.

Tuesday 23rd January. I was thinking the other night of a talk I heard over the wireless. A naval correspondent was talking about the duties of the Navy etcetera. We are doing everything he blahed about, yet it's just a matter of routine and we think nothing of it. It's a bit of a strain and we are always glad to get our heads down. The Repulse and Ark Royal are close at hand. When I go on watch in the middle of the night (12-4), clad only in a pair of shorts, I pity the folks back home putting extra clothing on and still shivering. We expect to be back in England about July or August (my estimation), so it won't be so bad for us. A lot of the lads are peeling badly or suffering from swollen legs and arms. At 13:00 hours today the sun was immediately overhead. At 18:15 hours sighted land. Put clock back 1 hour at 18:30. This is second time we have put clocks back. We are now 2 hours behind Greenwich mean time.

Wed 24th Jan. Saw my Service Certificate. Good reports. Keep on like that and I'll be alright. Nothing doing today, sun very hot, I'll be glad when it gets a bit cooler.

Thur 25th Jan. Got my wish today, some rain in the forenoon, definitely a bit cooler. Buzz going round we're for the Falkland Islands. Buzz number 2 Cape Town. Buzz 3 we're taking the Admiral home. But first we are going to pick up the Admiral and then, well, I favour the Falklands.

Friday 26th Jan. Sighted smoke 06:33. Overhauled ship 11:00. Friendly. MV Dunbar Castle Sunk by a mine outside Ramsgate. There was a pile of mail on her bound for Hawkins. Clock goes back one hour. Heavy rain today.

Sat 27th Jan. Nearly ran down Dutch ship during middle watch 03:00. Weather definitely cooler. Should pick Admiral up tomorrow. Bawled out by Physical Training Instructor and acting Petty Officer. He used to be in charge of the boys and I told him straight that he wasn't talking to a boy and told him also that I was looking forward to when he would invite me to the foc'sle for an exhibition boxing match. He refused to take the hint but he shut up. I'm going to lay for that bloke. Clocks go back another hour, 4 hours behind England now.

Officers of HMS Hawkins 1940

CHAPTER 4

28th January 1940

HMS Royal Oak Survivor's Tale

On the 14th of October 1939, at the same time as Ronnie was being target practice for the Navy on the South Coast, HMS Royal Oak became the first British battleship to be sunk in the war. Built for the First World War, Royal Oak was one of the Dreadnought's that took part in the Battle of Jutland. With four fifteen inch guns and fourteen six in guns, she packed a powerful punch.

At the start of the Second World War Royal Oak took part in the unsuccessful search for the German battleship Gneisenau. This was the beginning of the end for Royal Oak. Although heavily armed, the more modern ships were lighter and faster and she was now too slow to keep up with the rest of the fleet. Having been damaged by North Sea storms, she was sent to Scapa Flow in the Orkney's to provide anti aircraft cover for the anchorage.

A German reconnaissance flight over Scapa Flow prompted the Admiralty to disperse the bulk of the fleet from Scapa, leaving only a handful of ships for Royal Oak to guard. On a still, moonless night, illuminated only by the pale glow of the Northern Lights, the threat came not by air but from under the sea. The German U-Boat U-47, commanded by Captain Günther Prien, slipped past the sunken block ships guarding the Eastern entrance to the Flow and picked out Royal Oak as a sitting duck. Ronnie heard first hand about the disaster from a crewmate who survived the attack and raised some interesting questions about the events of that fatal night.

SUN 28TH JAN. SEEING A LOT OF FISH.

Sun 28th Jan. Seeing a lot of fish. During the first dog watch we saw flying fish, sharks, a seal, porpoise and a big ray. Pick up the Admiral tomorrow afternoon. We go overside tomorrow forenoon to paint the ship. Lifebelts will be worn. Overhauled another ship, trained guns on her until she identified herself. A Greek.

Had a long talk with a survivor of Royal Oak, the first battleship to be sunk in the war. The tale he told was pretty gruesome. My heart goes out to the boys who were aboard her. According to him the Royal Oak was never sunk by a torpedo. He says the explosion was internal and caused by explosives placed in stores. To clinch his argument he asks how a torpedo can get through a torpedo blister, 15 inches of armament and explode right in the centre of the ship. And if there was a submarine commander and crew with nerves strong enough to stand the strain of waiting 10 minutes after firing a fish to fire another one. He just fires the whole lot at once and beats it. Point two, a sub couldn't get into Scapa Flow. It was vivid, the tale he told. All the hands had turned in their hammocks when the explosion took place and all hands were mustered on deck, then for some reason the skipper told all hands except the emergency party to get below and turn in. About ten minutes later there was another explosion and the starboard side of the mess deck became a raging inferno. An oil bunker had exploded and the ship began to list. The hands below had been caught like rats in a trap, without a chance. The chap who told me about this said he walked down or along the ships side and over the blister to the drifter and he didn't see any sign of a rip suck, as a fish would have made. He and a lot more reckon it was the fuel tanks going up which caused her to sink.

Royal Oak Footnote:-

This eye witness account is a brilliant example of how even a primary historical source can be wrong in some of it's aspects. The survivor tells about how he walked down the side of the ship to a waiting drifter and didn't see any signs of a rupture to the Royal Oak's anti torpedo blister, (a cigar shaped armoured addition to the hull beneath the waterline). The truth is that he wouldn't have seen the torpedo damage. Photographs of the wreck show holes in the starboard side of the ship where the torpedo's struck. As sea water rushed in to the gaping holes the ship listed to starboard, so our survivor would only have been able to walk down the port side, where there was no torpedo damage.

He also recalled that the crew were called on deck when the ship was shaken by the first explosion. If they had abandoned ship at that point a great many lives would have been saved. Instead they were ordered below and subsequently trapped by massive explosions, fire and flooding from the open deck hatches and starboard portholes. Perhaps it is easy to see what should have been done with hindsight, but at the time the Captain and crew had no idea they were under attack. As our survivor confirmed, the belief was that no submarine could enter Scapa Flow, but the German's had planned the operation well. They knew that a U-Boat could slip past the block ships in Kirk Sound at high water and Dönitz had hand picked a Commander with the daring to pull it off.

The first explosion that night was Günther Prien's initial torpedo salvo. Two missed and one hit Royal Oak in the bow. The damage was below the waterline and not visible from the deck which contributed to the belief that there had been an explosion in the flammable stores in the bow. This would explain why the men were ordered below, while the explosion was investigated.

Günther Prien, contrary to expectation, did have the nerves of steel required to reload his torpedo tubes and have another go. This time all three hit home. The thick, anti-torpedo armour, carried by Royal Oak was designed to withstand World War 1 torpedoes. But technology had moved on and Prien's projectiles were bigger and more powerful, and ripped a massive hole in the hull and ignited cordite that sent a fireball through the mess decks.

The ship's tender, Daisy 2, had been moored on Royal Oak's port side. The captain of the tender, John Gatt, ordered Daisy 2 to be cut loose. Despite being caught by the lifting port side anti-torpedo blister, she was able to get free of the sinking ship and picked up 386 men from the water. Our survivor was extremely lucky to not only have escaped the carnage below decks but to be able to get into the drifter by walking down the hull. If he had been in the water, which was thick with choking fuel oil and bone chillingly cold, he may not have been so lucky. Such is the fine line between life and death in war. He owed his life to the drifter captain who kept his vessel next to a sinking, burning ship containing hundreds of tons of high explosives that could have blown apart at any time, an act of bravery for which he received the Distinguished Service Cross.

The next day the Navy sent down a local diver who was greeted by the gruesome site of a sea bed littered with bodies. Among the carnage he found the propellers of two torpedoes, confirming that Royal Oak had indeed been the victim of a submarine attack. However it would seem that this information didn't reach our survivor, who, as anyone deprived of the facts, filled in the gaps of the story with his own beliefs and conjecture.

The sinking of the Royal Oak was a major embarrassment to the government and a massive publicity coup for Hitler. Scapa Flow was the principle base for the British Navy in the North Sea and the German plan was to scatter the fleet out of it's base and allow themselves greater access to the Atlantic for the purposes of raiding Allied shipping and allowing supplies in, relieving the blockade. These twin aims mirrored the mission of HMS Hawkins, although Ronnie probably wouldn't have known this at the time, to protect shipping from German raiders and to maintain the blockade.

To a certain extent, the German plan worked. The Admiralty had already scattered the fleet from Scapa Flow in fear of a German raid. Germany probably thought a U-Boat attack on Scapa would be like shooting fish in a barrel. As it was, the pickings were slim but the end result for Germany was achieved. They also gained some revenge for the surrender and scuttling of their fleet in Scapa Flow after the First World War.

The consensus seemed to be that the British were happy to let the Germans take the credit for a daring U-Boat raid because it distracted from deficiencies in the defensive set-up of Scapa Flow. Diverting attention to the daring of the German U-Boat commander was politically a much better outcome. The government however, did shut the stable door after the horse had bolted and erected the Churchill Barriers across Kirk Sound to stop any further access to the anchorage via that route.

Out of a crew of 1,234 men and boys, 834 lives were lost, many of them boys under 18. A fact that altered Naval policy thereafter in regards to how many boys would be part of a ships company. As well as those who went down with the ship, others perished in the cold, oil covered waters. Some managed to swim the 800 metres to shore but many of them perished shortly after. The wreck lies almost upside down in 100ft of water and is now a designated war grave.

It's hard to imagine the courage of shipwrecked sailors, particularly those who survived the horror of being torpedoed. Not only to escape with their lives but to then go back into action. Like a boxer who is knocked down and gets up again, they just want to finish the fight.

CHAPTER 5
29th January 1940

Battle of the River Plate - HMS Ajax Survivor Story

January 1940 was bang in the middle of the period dubbed 'the phoney war', so called because hostilities on land hadn't got going with any kind of serious intent. Germany had invaded Poland but Britain and France in response had sat on their hands in terms of taking the fight to the aggressor, their main efforts being directed towards hasty rearmament.

The war at sea however was anything but phoney. Within hours of war being declared the British liner SS Athenia was torpedoed off the Hebrides with the loss of 112 lives. Then just two weeks later on the 14th of September 1939 the aircraft carrier HMS Courageous was torpedoed by U-29 off the coast of Ireland, ironically while on anti-submarine patrol. She capsized and sank in just twenty minutes with the loss of 519 crew. In October the Royal Oak was sunk with the loss of 834 lives. Three nil to the Germans and nearly 1500 dead. Britain and its allies badly needed a victory of some sort and with nothing happening on land it had to come from the war at sea.

Ironically Britain was falling victim to the restrictions it had forced on Germany following the First World War. The Treaty of Versailles severely restricted Germany's ability to build up a Navy of conspicuous surface vessels. Instead they concentrated on building U-Boats and a handful of small but powerful cruisers or 'pocket battleships' which were under the 10,000 ton limit of the Treaty. Germany knew they couldn't match the combined allied navies when it came to a stand-up fight so they concentrated on building a force for Commerce Raiding. The philosophy of Admiral Dönitz, the commander of the German Navy, was that for every merchant ship sunk another would have to be built to replace it: a double hit. So long as the Germans were able to sink ships faster than they could be replaced, then the strategy would be successful. They were not restricted to any theatre of war and although the bulk of U-Boat activity was in the North Atlantic, armed merchantmen (auxiliary cruisers) and heavy cruisers could take the tonnage war to the far corners of the globe.

The pick of the pocket battleships was Admiral Graf Spee, commanded by KzS Hans Langsdorff. She was looking to take prizes from the East Indies and Arabian Gulf shipping route and was patrolling the waters around South Africa.

The Graf Spee, had set sail in August 1939 bound for the South Atlantic. Armed with six 11 inch guns and with a top speed of 28 knots she was designed to outgun any ship fast enough to catch her (like Hawkins, top speed 30 knots) and was fast enough to outrun any ship big enough to inflict serious damage. Between September and December 1939 she took-out nine merchant ships in the South Atlantic and Indian Ocean.

Unlike U-Boats who's only tactic was to sink their target, the mere presence of the Graf Spee was sufficient to take a merchantman out of the war. Operating under 'Prize Rules', which state that crews of merchant ships should be in a place of safety (this doesn't mean life boats, unless close to land) before sinking. The Graf Spee's captain Hans Langsdorff would either transfer crews to his ship or to his supply ship the Altmark, then sink the vessel either by gunfire or demolition charges.

Langsdorff's last prize, on December 7th, was the freighter Streonshalh, from which he obtained secret documents relating to shipping routes. Based on this information he decided to head west towards Montevideo and the River Plate, where he hoped to encounter a convoy.

The last two ships taken by Graf Spee managed to get a signal off before being destroyed and from this information Commodore Henry Harwood worked out, with a combination of a sea dogs intuition (as Ronnie might have put it) and simple maths, where Graf Spee would be headed next.

The Graf Spee was such a menace that the British and French navies gathered a force of four aircraft carriers, three battleships and sixteen cruisers to hunt her down. One part of that cohort was Force G, under the charge of Commodore Henry Harwood.

Force G comprised two heavy cruisers Cumberland and Exeter and the light cruisers Ajax and the New Zealand ship HMNZS Achilles. The Admiralty had directed Harwood to patrol the eastern coast of South America.

Because of the pattern of Graf Spee's recent raids, Harwood reasoned she was heading towards South America to further attack the shipping lanes from either the River Plate or Rio de Janeiro and also possibly to make a revenge attack for the heavy German naval defeat in the First World War Battle of the Falklands. The beginning of December 1939 was the 25th anniversary of the defeat of the Pocket Battleship's namesake Admiral Graf Spee who was the commander of a German raid on Port Stanley in the Falkland Islands in December 1914.

Harwood dispatched HMS Cumberland to the Falklands and kept the other three ships on patrol outside the River Plate. His estimates were correct. As dawn broke on 13th of December the Graf Spee lookout spotted two tall masts on the horizon. Langsdorf identifying the ship as HMS Exeter, assumed she was escorting a convoy and gave orders to bring the ship to attack speed. The Graf Spee had steamed over 30,000 miles since leaving Germany and her 56,000 horsepower diesels were badly in need of a refit. A great plume of black smoke from the engines on full throttle alerted the British to her presence and the first major naval battle since Jutland was on.

Six weeks after the battle, Ronnie was able to get a first hand account of all the gory details, from one of the crew of HMS Ajax.

MONDAY 29TH JAN. SIGHT TANKER AT DAWN.

Monday 29th Jan. Sight tanker at dawn. Achilles about 15 minutes later. No mail. Admiral aboard tanker. Several ratings from Ajax and Achilles come aboard as ships company. Talking to a chap from Ajax and he gave me an account of the battle of the River Plate. The Exeter was disabled 12 minutes after the first shot was fired and the Ajax was also badly battered. The Achilles only lost 7 men. She was the lucky one. I'll try and give it as he told me.

"I'd just turned in when the rattlers (Action Stations alarm) went. I ran to my action station and was looking around for the cause of the alarm, when boom! And the sea seemed to boil. I saw the flash as the Exeter fired and then another crash and the Exeter seemed enveloped in flames. Next I knew we were hard at it. I don't remember much of the actual fight, just working the guns. Suddenly a shell landed near us. It was hell. Mess mates of mine, full of life, joking and laughing as they did their job, next second they were shapeless forms lying on the deck or bits of flesh and blood splattered all over the place, ourselves included. Others were lying around in agony waiting for assistance. Boom! Another salvo and our gun is wiped out. I'm lucky I only got hit in the knee, just above the knee cap. The sick bay Tiffie came along and yanked a piece of steel outa my leg and sewed and bandaged it up. I went back to my gun but it was damaged beyond repair and a clearing up party were throwing the bodies overboard and taking others to the sick bay, where they were patched up and if possible sent back to action. Some of the lads, badly wounded as they were, wanted to get back

into action and they were hard pressed to keep them in sick bay. I went along to the forrad gun but was knocked out on the way there by a head wound. The aftermath was the worst, when the heat of battle abated and realization came. 27 men went mad. Stark staring raving mad. Happily they are alright now. We finished the battle with one gun in action and that was manned mostly by boys. The ship was a shambles, we certainly bore the brunt of the battle and we have the Admiral to thank for being afloat. He was as cool as a cucumber, even timing the firing of the Spee. After we chased the Spee into Montivideo we had time to square up a bit. There was a lot printed in the papers about the Ark Royal and Repulse and a battleship waiting for her, but it isn't true. The only ships waiting for her were the Ajax and Achilles and Ajax only had one gun fit for action, it was a good bit of bluff. Had the Graf Spee come out fighting she would have wiped us up. After the battle a lot of chaps were even scared to put to sea. Their nerves were shot all to pieces. I've had my bellyful of fighting and I'm not a coward, but when 11 inch shells come screaming at you, well I know why the Navy supply two pairs of pants."

River Plate Footnote:-

The damage to Harwood's ships was immense. Exeter was severely damaged and as our sailor recounted, Ajax and Achilles were also all but out for the count. Graf Spee was a modern ship, only launched in 1936 whereas the British ships were at least ten years older, having been built in the First World War. The German ship had all the latest gunnery technology, state of the art radar and shell sizes twice as big as the British.

HMS Ajax

Crucero Británico ACHILLES

HMNZS Achilles

Harwood's brilliant battle management and the sheer tenacity of the allied crews combined to give their superior opponent a mauling. Graf Spee having been hit at least seventy times, broke off the engagement and took refuge in the neutral Uruguayan port of Montevideo. Langsdorf, believing British reinforcements were on the way decided to save his crew from further losses and to prevent the ship falling into the hands of British Intelligence, (Uruguay was sympathetic to the British), he scuttled the Graf Spee in the River Plate estuary, and later committed suicide rather than return to Germany dishonoured. Commodore Harwood, on the other hand, was promoted to Rear Admiral and knighted.

German Casualties from the Graf Spee

Graf Spee Scuttled in the River Plat

The Battle of the River Plate was a tremendous morale boosting victory for the British early in the war. A much needed reply to the sinking of HMS Royal Oak. So much so that Hollywood later made a feature film of the battle with Anthony Quayle playing Admiral Harwood.

The picture of the battle painted by the sailor from the Ajax was far more horrific than could be portrayed in a 1956 film. You might think the Ajax seaman's gory tail might have tempered Ronnie's appetite for action, but the brutal and bloody truth of war only seemed to make him want it more.

CHAPTER 6

30th January to 9th February 1940

Chats with the Admiral

At first Ronnie was sceptical of having the Admiral on board, rather like having the head teacher sitting in on school lessons. Visions of extra scrubbing, polishing and generally having to behave yourself wouldn't have appealed to Ronnie's rebellious spirit. But Admiral Harwood obviously had quite a bit of charisma about him. He certainly seems to have charmed Ronnie. Getting all the men together to tell them his version of the Battle of the River Plate, not bawling out Ronnie and his mates for lying down on the job, and taking time to chat on a personal level - comparing tattoos, all touches of leadership genius guaranteed to get the men on his side.

Harwood's approach shows that he was aware of how much stress was involved in crewing a battle cruiser in a war zone. He'd witnessed men being blown apart and turning into raving lunatics and he knew that when not actively engaging the enemy there were hours and hours of tense inactivity just waiting for something to happen. Little touches like allowing the men to rig a canvas swimming pool on deck, letting the crew write home about their shore visits and changing the watch timings to allow more sleep were the small details which made life more bearable.

The constant painting and repainting of the ship was probably also a subtle way of making work for idle hands as well as a strategic and physical necessity. It also gave Ronnie time to contemplate the possibility of a fight the next time they were in port.

TUESDAY 30TH JAN. WE ARE ON OUR
WANDERINGS ONCE MORE

Tuesday 30th Jan. We are on our wanderings once more. We sailed monday night and the wind is gradually rising, I'm afraid we are in for a storm. I'm getting a trifle fed up from the routine and the ship. Two hours leave since we left Pompey on 27th December and there is none in sight yet. Bit of excitement tonight, a fire in the first cutter, soon put it out.

Wed 31st Jan. We are getting paid today and after this payment we are getting paid once a month. Saw the Admiral at close quarters today. We were lying down on the gun platform when he came along the catwalk. We jumped to attention but he told us to resume our positions and get as much rest as we could, so long we didn't go to sleep. Decent bloke. Typical sea dog.

In the near future we are doing 36 hours manoeuvres with the Shropshire. We eat, sleep and make merry by the gun, not leaving it once. By all accounts we are on a fourteen day patrol and then putting in to Rio de Janeiro for fuel, and only fuel, no leave! If they are not careful they will have trouble. The lads are rumbling. It's now blowing a gale and it will increase in force as time draws on. It is very cold and we are still in tropical gear. We wrap up well when we go on watch. I wish we would get some mail. The Admiral, I noticed, is tattooed.

Admiral Sir Henry Harwood OBE

Thur 1st Feb. Just another day. The weather has calmed and its getting hot again. When the Admiral came aboard he had the clocks put on two hours. You see we have action stations morning and night, dawn and dusk and we are having to turn out about 04:20 and if we'd had the middle watch we'd have only been relieved twenty minutes previous (04:00) and we weren't getting any sleep. So he's altered that and now we get about six hours sleep, if we're lucky. A lot of chaps, myself included, don't bother slinging their hammocks, we just get down on the deck with our oilskins under us and our life belts as a pillow and we're off. 22:50 was sitting on ammunition seat on gun with earphones on when I saw a meteorite fall. It lit up the whole sky.

Fri Feb 1st. The Admiral summoned us all on the quarter deck and spun us a yarn. He told us the facts about the Graf Spee scrap. The Exeter's Bridge was blown clean away and everybody killed bar the skipper. The Ajax had seven hits on her and one went right through and landed in the admirals bunk, where it exploded. He told us one fact I must record. In his own words. "Having been straddled twelve times and hit seven times we were in rather a bad way. So I gave the order to retire. We laid smoke screens and retired and to our relief, so did the Spee."

Sat Feb 3rd. The Dorsetshire and Shropshire 8 inch cruisers contacted us at dawn and we carried out exercises. They will be with us till monday. We were to do a shoot but we ran into a tropical rain storm so it was abandoned. All R.C. piped to give their names. Suspect Admiral is an R.C. I have been appointed auxiliary trainer for 7.5 gun, in case trainer is killed. Five U-Boats in the vicinity.

Sun Feb 4th. Cruisers still with us. Admiral inspected us and asked everybody who he was and what he did outside. Then he took us R.C's for Service in his cabin.

Monday Feb 5th. Cruisers left us at noon. At 08:40 we ran through a school of whales. I counted 32 and 1 shark. Appendicitis case operated on, operation a success. Senior MO is a Harley Street doctor.

Tuesday 6th Feb. Expect to be in Rio de Janeiro on the 12th of Feb. Rig will be white duck suits. Had a chat with Admiral. Was sentry on the aft 4 inch HA gun when he came along. He compliments me on my choice of tattoos and the distinctiveness of them. He liked the tiger. He asked me who I was and where I was from. We have to have sentries on all guns and magazines as somebody had been tampering with them. The Admiral also told me he was very pleased with the condition of the ship and seeing the majority of ratings were reserve men, more so. Rigged swimming bath on upper deck. First in! Boy was it "gorgus". Painting ship today, or should I say scraping. Passed a ship - Portugese.

HMS Hawkins improvised swimming pool

Wed 7th Feb. Painting ship dark grey until ship leaves Rio. Then we paint her light grey. Passed another ship last night, we were 40 miles from Rio. This morning the ship is full of butterflies and moths and birds and insects.

Thursday 8th Feb. We are now able to write and tell the folks which ports we touch, providing they are not British owned. The Admiral gave permission and he said, "the lads have little enough to write about and as the newspapers will print photos etc they may as well let their people at home know where they are." The South American ports are lousy with Germans and we been warned not to provoke fights or be provoked. But the bloke said if you do fight, fight clean and hit hard.

Friday Feb 9th. A German oil tanker left port yesterday but hearing we were in the vicinity she put back into harbour.

CHAPTER 7

10th to 14th February 1940

Ronnie Does Rio

After a month at sea the routine of ship life was beginning to bed in and when Ronnie wasn't on duty by the gun or painting the ship or comparing tattoos with the Admiral, he must have had a lot of time to think about his two biggest preoccupations, mail from home and shore leave.

Rio de Janeiro would be Ron's first taste of South America and the taste was steak! Prime Brazilian rump must have been a welcome change from ships rations and a far cry from holiday camp fare. Rio, even today, has a tremendously exotic feel to it. As a kid I remember being fascinated by a pill box decorated with iridescent blue butterfly wings that Ron brought back from Rio for my mum, his sister Josie.

If it was a big deal for Ron visiting Rio it was the same for Rio having a visit from the Navy. Even Pathé news (https://youtu.be/-BvscUmTCYs) covered the event. Following his victory over the Graf Spee, Admiral Harwood was quite a celebrity and his flagship putting into port generated lots of interest. I wonder if the folks back home were craning their necks in the cinema to catch a glimpse of Ron in his white duck suit?

Sat 10th Feb. Usual routine, we will put into Rio

Sat 10th Feb. Usual routine, we will put into Rio de Janerio Monday 12th, shore leave will be granted. We will be there 48 hours. I'm wondering if I can borrow a white cap anywhere, otherwise I won't get any leave.

Sunday - White Ducks, shore rig. Placed all wires for tying up, expect oiler alongside early Monday morning.

Mon Feb 12th 04:00hrs, relieved middle watch, take over morning watch. 04:50 exercise action stations. Both watches secure. We went down to breakfast and clean into rig of the day. When we were piped to fall in for Cruising Stations, we got the guns ready for action and then the alarm sounded. At this time we were only a half hour steaming from port. We closed up around the guns and the ship making a turn of 180 degrees picked up speed. Within an hour we were going full out 30 knots. We got news that as we were coming in one *side of the harbour, round a pile of islands, a German oil tanker had slipped out the other side. We kept up speed all day and at 14:30 we received news that HMS Dorsetshire's plane had sighted her and she set fire to herself. We made off back to Rio and expect to get there tonight. We could see the smoke on the horizon. I wish we'd met her. But I suppose she would have scuttled herself before we could get to her. The boarding party and prize crew were all ready. As we entered the harbour there is a big figure of Christ and a big crucifix. I thought we were in for a bit of fun. The name of the tanker was Wakama. We were nearer to her than the Dorsetshire when she set fire to herself but we only had fuel for another eight hours steaming and we wanted to catch the tide.*

Tuesday 13th. Rio de Janeiro, Monday.We dropped our hook at about 7pm and piped Liberty Men. So I changed into white ducks as I was watch ashore. We landed on the quay about eight o'clock and were warmly greeted by the people gathered there. I had no companion as my mates were watch aboard. My first job was to get some money changed and then made a beeline for the nearest cafe. I ordered food, just like that, "food". The waiter seemed to understand, he dashed away and brought back a bottle of iced beer. It looked too tempting to refuse and boy was it good, the first cold drink I'd had in a month. Then I had a good feed of steak and eggs and finished off with real coffee. Then I went to the Europa Hotel and booked a room for the night, 10 mille-real, about 2/6d, there was no boat aboard that night. I went sight seeing when I'd finished those prelims. There is a giant statue of Christ. I found that and a church but I couldn't get hold of a priest. Rio is a fine modern city. I went to the movies but the stink drove me out. I was picked up by a party of Yanks and went for a taxi ride finishing up in a hotel with a floor show. Then I made tracks for bed and ran into a crowd of our blokes being photographed for a newspaper, so I joined them. I have a paper in my case. It's not a bad picture. I bought a few curios and views and retired for the night. In the morning I caught the 7 o'clock boat back to the ship. Immediately the last liberty men were aboard we raised anchor and tied up alongside the quay and the oilers came alongside. Before we moved from our anchorage we fired a salute of 21 guns

and received 19 in return. We cleaned
ship and the stores started coming
aboard, boy did we work. At 1-30pm the
liberty men went ashore. I was one of the
watch aboard. We worked all afternoon and
evening getting provisions aboard and
keeping an eye on the oilers.

Wed 14th Feb. No leave today. All
hands to turn to and provision ship. I
don't think it's worth coming into port,
we work too damned hard. We had just
finished provisioning when a lorry
stacked high with cases of apples. We
were wild. Winesap's they were. However,
we unloaded them with a will when we were
told that they were a present from the
British residents to the crew. We had
about 20 apples each. We sailed about 4pm
and were met just outside the harbour by
the Dorsetshire. She will keep us company
for four days for range finding exercise.
While we were in Rio the canteen
committee bought £40-0-0 worth of records
out of the canteen fund, also some
clocks.

Rio de Janeiro

CHAPTER 8

15th to 29th Feb 1940

Letters From Home

Ronnie had his wish for shore leave granted but there was still no sign of mail from home. The role of mail in keeping up morale was well known to military high command. Later in the war the Americans even went so far as to devise what was probably the paper precursor of email called v-mail. These one sided lettergrams were photographed onto micro film, transported by plane, then printed at destination. Airmail was much faster than by ship and letters on film saved a huge amount of space as you could get 18,000 letters on one film reel.

But in the early days of the war, letters still went by ship, and three months into their patrol the lads on Hawkins were still waiting for their precious letters from home. Perhaps the captain realised that the men might have too much time to think of home and kept them busy with cleaning and painting the ship.

It's not clear from Ronnie's writing how much they knew about their role in the overall pattern of the war, but the power of the British Navy was crucial in keeping the country fed and supplied. In World War Two there were 19.5 million military deaths but an estimated 20 million died of starvation. Incidentally the ration of the average American GI was nearly 5000 calories a day, more than one and a half times the level of British rationing of 3000 calories per day for a man.

Argentina, Brazil and Uruguay exported beef, grain and raw materials to sustain the war effort. The presence of British warships in the Atlantic was keeping those supply lines open and also cutting off supplies to

Germany. Every enemy ship that got away could be used against the allies in the future. For example Ronnie mentions that the Antonio Delphino slipped out of Bahia and got away. This vessel was later used as a U-Boat supply ship.

THUR FEB 15TH CLEANING SHIP.

Thur Feb 15th Cleaning ship. Usual routine, Dorsetshire is still with us, she has prisoners of German ship on board.

Fri Feb 16th. Mother's Birthday. Painting ship a light grey. I wonder when this war will finish.

Sat 17th. Same as usual. P & O boat an A.M.C. sighted us and cleared away for action. She thought we was a German cruiser. Did we laff.

Sun 18th Feb. Division. Short service in Admirals cabin. Dorsetshire still with us. We may take Jerry aboard.

Monday 19th Feb. Nothing doing today. Very warm.

Tue 20th Feb. Dorsetshire still with us. Contacted Albatross an A.M. Cruiser. Kept company with her for half a day. About 17:00 we overtook Liverpool meat steamer Upton Grange. We are supposed to sight Queen of Bermuda sometime this week and there is a strong buzz there is mail aboard for us.

Wed 21st Feb. Dorsetshire still with us. Doing a full calibre shoot shortly. Still painting ship, leaving hull a dark grey and rest of ship a dark grey.

Thurs 22nd Feb. We sighted Queen of Bermuda approximately 21:00 but we lost her as darkness fell and a rainstorm blew up. Sighted her at midnight and lowered a boat. She has no mail for us and she brought money for our next payment. We are patrolling the traffic lanes from Rio. Keeping an eye on our shipping. Also we are waiting for a German, the Windhoese of 16,000 tons. She'll be a rich prize if we can get her. At present we are off Cape Frio, close to where the Wakhama scuttled herself. The German liner is in Santos.

Friday 23rd Feb. Leaving the Rio area for River Plate. German ship Antonio Dolfino slipped out of port and got away. She was too far north for us to chase her. Bahia was the port she was in. Leaving her to the northern patrol. We are going to take Jerries on board for two days as the Dorsetshire is going into Montevideo for fuelling. Our next port of call may be BA (Buenos Aries) or Falkland Isles.

Sat 24th Feb. Full calibre shoot 7.5 gun.

HMS Hawkins Full Calibre Shoot

Six rounds per gun. It was a throw off shoot with Dorsetshire as target. All sights are "fixed" to six degrees of elevation. We train the gun on the Dorsetshire and fire at her but the shells all fall astern. We are outside the trade routes at present.

Sunday 25th Feb. Quiet day. Sunday routine. Disturbed whales. Big school of them. Albatross following ship. Porpoise playing about. Very hot.

Monday Feb 26th. Sighted oiler. Wind getting up. Blowing half a gale. Arrangements to take over prisoners. Dorsetshire going into Montevideo for refuel etc. Wind still strong. Expect her to bring mail for us.

Tuesday 27th Feb. Lookouts report darkened ship. Gave chase. She turned out to be the Dunster Grange, one of Holder's boats homeward bound for Liverpool. We intended to oil early on Monday but the weather was rough. The Dorsetshire was to give us the prisoners and take our mail. She however has gone to the Falklands as she couldn't wait any longer for oil and she couldn't put into a neutral port with prisoners aboard. The delay in getting our mail is however a blessing in disguise as a mailboat is due in today and therefore we may get a fortnight's mail extra.

Wednesday 28th Feb. We are in contact with oiler Olwen. Weather is still rough. We are going into the River Plate for shelter. Cruising up and down outside Montevideo waiting for oiler to come out, she went in for shelter. 18:00 hours sighted wreck of Graf Spee.

Thursday 29th Feb. At nine o'clock approximately last night we sighed a small tug heading for us. Immediately all glasses and telescopes were trained on her a buzz went round the ship. She has mail for us. Nobody believed it, there had been so many false alarms. As she drew nearer some of the keener eyes verified the fact that she had bags of some sort stowed abaft the funnel. Then she turned broadside to us and everyone aboard broke into huge grins. They were unmistakably mail bags. There were plenty of volunteers to carry the bags to the rec space where they were immediately sorted. I got thirteen letters, two lots of everybodies and three Weekly Post's.

Peace and quiet during forenoon watch, everybody happy and busy with mail. Sighted fleet Argentine Navy during first dock watch and fired salute. Payed last night.

Letters from Home

CHAPTER 9

2nd to 5th Mar 1940

Montevideo or bust

Uruguay was Ronnie's second South American country in successive months and I'm sure he couldn't wait to get a Montevideo badge for his anorak. In true Turner fashion he made a beeline for "food" with no doubt the unwritten subtext of "drink". Even 75 years later you can almost smell the boozy breath of his shore leave photo's. He was a sailor and a scouser, what more could you expect! By the way, Scousers don't take offence (calm down, calm down) I'm writing this as a Liverpudlian born and bred. I'm not pandering to the stereotype, just speaking from experience!

Perhaps careful that his diary might fall into the disapproving hands of his mother on return home, he makes sure to mention he is at least trying to keep his Catholic end up if not always successfully.

Uruguay, like many South American countries, had a population that derived mostly from Europe. Montevideo, the Uruguayan capital, had a thriving British community with a number of British associations and clubs dedicated to all things Blighty, from Queen Mary's Needlework Guild to the British Schools Old Boys Club. They must have been thrilled to have a British warship in port and what better way to contribute to the war effort than a lorry load of apples for the crew... load them yourself though boys!

SAT MARCH 2ND. USUAL ROUTINE. FULL
CALIBRE GUN DRILL

Sat March 2nd. Usual routine. Full calibre gun drill shoot. South American reported heavy gun fire off coast and big naval battle. Oiled.

Sunday March 3rd. Sunday routine. On track route mail closes 4pm 16:00 hours. My my every bodies writing. I wrote eleven letters myself.

Monday. We are going into Montevideo for a 24 hour visit. 4pm the clocks put back two hours to 2pm and get ship ready for tying up. Arrived Monte 2pm, clean for shore. Landed liberty men about 05:30. Buses were waiting for us on the quay provided by the British Settlement Committee for the British seamen. Buses ran to the headquarters in the town and also to the beaches. Went to their headquarters and had a good meal. Then went around sight seeing. Everybody was glad to see us. Monte is a bigger place than Rio with more English people. We (three of us) had our photographs taken. Inadvertently we went into the children's section. We didn't worry though. We picked up dolls that were lying around and got taken with em. 2/- each they cost, one each, dear but good.

Shore Leave Montevideo

Then I took em to the St Helens Club (Apostleship of the Sea). They were scared about going but I prevailed upon them as I wanted to see the priest. When we got there the priest was crowded with the boys. They'll be taken sight seeing and then invited there for tea, the Parson with them. The priest was absent, he'd gone to Paraguay for some reason and they had sold out of Apostleship of the Sea prayer books. We had a nice time there and then we went on to a dance. The dance was given by the British people and was free with free beer and wines and spirits. The dance finished about 2 o'clock. We got a taxi back to ship. We enjoyed ourselves.

Tue 5th March. Found watch aboard had provisioned ship night before. Larked around generally dodging the work. 2pm fell in for leaving harbour, Band playing.

CHAPTER 10
6th to 15th Mar 1940

Expensive beer in the Falklands

The Falklands was Ronnie's third country in three weeks. By this time he was becoming an expert at sniffing out free meals from the locals who by the looks of it, gave with one hand and took back with the other, judging by Ron's disgust at the price of beer.

Port Stanley had long been an important place for sailors. Much of its early prosperity was as a ship repair base for vessels damaged from savage weather while rounding the Horn. HMS Exeter took refuge and repairs there following the battle of the River Plate, with several of the crew who didn't make it buried on the island. For the Navy in World War Two, it was an important supply base for refuelling and provisioning. With five of the Hawkins ratings falling into the harbour drunk, it was obviously an important refuelling stop for the sailors as well.

WEDNESDAY 6TH. WE ARE GOING TO FALKLAND ISLES.

Wednesday 6th. We are going to Falkland Isles. Usual ships routine. Picked up lifebelt, no name or mark on it. Getting colder.

Thurs Mar 7th. Colder still. Sammy coats issued. Believe will be at Falklands for 5 days. Paravanes out going through own minefields.

Friday March 8th. Our letters posted in Rio should be in our home today. Middle watch, bitterly cold. We arrive Port Stanley 07:00, weather a bit warmer now sun has risen. This place is forlorn and lonely very like some of the barren Isles off the Scottish coast. There isn't a tree in sight. We picked up the Admirals barge here. I've been made one of the barge's crew. Oiler Sun Coaster came alongside early and we filled up. Later in the day a drifter unloaded flour. We paint over the side tomorrow.

Sat March 9th. Postponed painting ship. Went ashore, had a good meal with real fresh eggs. Walked around, nothing to see. Went to cemetery, chaps who died of wounds are buried there.

Crew from HMS Exeter buried on Falklands

Invited into a house and had tea there, very pleasant people. Fresh beef 4d a lb and they called it dear. Most things are double the price they are in England.

Sun Mar 10. Provisioning and stores work. No Church Parade.

Mon Mar 11. Washing ship side. Painting tomorrow.

Tues Mar 12th. Painting ships side. The Jimmy (First Officer) promised us a pipe down when we finished it. Ships side painted in record time. Piped down 14:00. Had a good bath and did some dobying. Both very necessary as I have had no time since entering harbour.

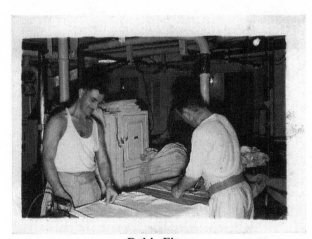

Dobie Firm

We are supposed to be in here for a rest but we have worked harder and longer than ever. Tomorrow we wash funnels and paint superstructure. Went ashore 5pm and watched soccer match. Visited church, St Mary's. Nuns invited me to tea at their guest house. Nice tea. Found priest's house, found him in. Had a long talk. Selesian order, he comes from St Helen's Lancs.

Mon 13th Wed. Rigged chains for funnel. Washed funnels and paintwork. While we've been here five ratings have fallen into the drink from the drifter which takes us ashore (drunk). The beer is very strong here and very dear price it is, 7d a glass, 1/8 a pint bottle. Put flat sweeper soon got on upper deck again. Told P.O. I was an Able Seaman not a domestic servant.

Thur Mar 14th. Securing ship for sea. Wind blowing up. Sent postcard off. Everything on this island is double the price. Clean ship, too wild to paint funnel.

Fri March 15th. My Birthday and I think it's the first I've spent away from home. I wonder what they are thinking at home? It's very cold down here but not as cold as it is in England. We caught the tail end of their summer. We were supposed to go to sea today but it was too wild. If weather moderates we will sail tomorrow morning at 6:30. Been keeping anchor watches in case ship drags anchor (Helmsman).

Cold weather off the Falklands

CHAPTER 11

16th Mar to 12th Apr 1940

Painting, storms and back to Monte

Ronnie was an experienced sailor. He started life at sea as a Bell Boy on the SS Minnedosa when he was fourteen, on the run from Liverpool to Nova Scotia, so a little rough weather was nothing he couldn't handle.

However in 1940, Gore-Tex was still a long way off and being wet was an occupational hazard for a wartime sailor. The 4" gun that Ronnie had to sit by was in a position exposed to the elements between the two funnels. Some of his photos show Hawkins crashing through huge waves that would have thrown spray right over the ship, soaking anyone on deck.

Ronnie as a Bell Boy on the SS Minnedosa age 14

If armed German raiders and Atlantic storms weren't enough to contend with, the Navy added it's own dangerous sport of painting the funnels in a gale.

Health and Safety regulations were also waiting to be invented. Having said that, Ron was issued with anti-flash gear to protect him from burning discharges from the gun. The downside is that they were made from asbestos: I suppose they meant well!

For these four weeks in March and April 1940, Hawkins was patrolling up the South American Coast from the Falklands to Rio Grande du Sol in Southern Brazil, about 400 miles or so, ending up back in Montevideo to top up on spuds, meat and mail. I love the image in my head of Ron sloping off painting duties and hiding over the side, sitting on the anchor, to read his letters in peace.

*S*AT *16 M*ARCH. *S*AILED. *W*EATHER DIRTY,
SEAS MOUNTAINOUS

Sat 16 March. Sailed. Weather dirty, seas mountainous though calmer than day before.

No Shelter from the Elements

Closed up at action stations as soon as we left harbour. Soon slipped into old routine. I hate going into port as we have to work all day and everyday and work hard. One compensation is that we have all night in our hammocks. We had a Starshell practice shoot at dusk (night action station) it was too misty to be effective.

Sunday 17. All Ireland St Patricks. Very quiet day. Attended a service in Admirals cabin. Palm Sunday gospel. A few of the lads had a sing song.. Quiet day. Weather wild and if anything, cold. We had turkey for dinner.

Monday 18th March. Seas still wild. This ship's a damn good sea boat. Winds are warmer. Holystoning the deck for a fortnight to bring em white. I'm going to get out of that lot if poss. I don't like going down on my hands and knees.

Tues 19th March. On hands and knees holystoning, was on watch yesterday morning and so missed it. Had a chat with Chief in Commanders office. Upshot of it is he put me in the Side Party. I think I'll miss further holystoning. Side party look after ship's side, keeping it clean and looking after booms etc. And also we look after the incinerator.

Wed 20th March. A young stoker got caught in the engines. Regret to say he died about two hours later and was buried at sea at Evening Quarters. Nothing else doing.

Thur 21st March. Quiet day. Seas running high. Storm brewing.

Fri 22 Mar. Storm. Seas mountain high. Running into Montevideo for mail. Expect to receive it 7:30 Sat. Weather calmer in the Plate.

Sat 23rd. Received mail 07:30 this morn. I got six letters, three Weekly Post's, three Daily Mirror's and two lots of everybodies. (Shush reading.)

Reading Time

Sun Easter 24th March. Service in Admirals cabin. Closed up during forenoon. Weather vile. I haven't been dry for a week.

Mon 25th March. Rigged chains on funnel for Stages and Bosuns chairs. Nearly got blown off. I had to climb around the top of funnels and reeve heaving lines through blocks. The chain is made fast and pulled thru'. There is no foothold and one has to hang on by the hands. As she had a 20 degree roll on her it was very unpleasant. Paint tomorrow.

Thursday 26th March. Seas heavy. Painting washed out. Did a bit of scraping. Everything battened down and lashed secure. 50 mile an hour gale blowing.

Rough Weather

Wed 27th March. Dirty night, issued with oilskins, sou'wester, pants and coat. Rain stopped and sea still wild. Started painting.

Thur 28th March. Seas going down. Something in the air. Training extra gun crews. Suspect aircraft. One sighted and identified as a Jerry. Three German in the vicinity. Expect to arrive Buenos A Monday. No shore leave except in organised parties. Big pro German community. British residents to do the honours.

Fri March 29. Painting ship funnels and superstructure and guns. Sea a flat calm. Hot weather again. There is a strong buzz we expect to be home in May.

Painting the Funnels

Sat 30th March. Pay day, very welcome. Cruising around Rio Grande we bottled a German ship up in there. She's a twin funnelled 12,000 tonner and caries a plane (mail) and is believed to be armed with 6 inch guns.

Sunday March 31st. Just our luck we have to oil and we're meeting the oiler at the River Plate. The chances are that Jerry will escape while we are away.

Monday 1st April. Sighted oiler at dawn and she came alongside almost at once. Arndale is the oiler's name. We fuelled in record time and at 12:00 we were headed back to the Rio Grande at a full 25 knots. She's still in port.

Tue 2nd April. No B.A. For us this trip. Presidents wife very ill. Run out of spuds and fresh meat. Weather sunny.

Wed 4th April. Nothing much doing. Might go to Monte again. Jerry ship believed interned. I'm not going to write much unless it's of interest. Stokers effects sold, realised £25-10-0 and only half sold. Navy doesn't allow subscriptions so they auction the dead man's effects and they are usually sold over and over again. The boys buy em and put em back.

Thur 5th April. Issued with anti flash gear. Hood to cover head and shoulders and elbow length gloves of asbestos.

Thur 11th April. I haven't kept the diary up to date because I wish to conserve paper. The 6th, 7th and 8th April was just the usual routine. On the 8th April we put into Montevideo for food and stores. We were well received and had a real good time.

Ron (right) and pals refreshed in Montevideo

We were allowed 48 hours stay and this time I didn't do much work. I was side party and we had to paint the anchors. Another bloke and I were going over the side when they gave the mail out. I collected mine and went over the side and made myself comfortable on the anchor and read my letters. When I'd finished reading, then I decided to start work. Took my time and finished the day feeling quite fresh.

Friday 12th April. Did very little work this afternoon. Changed and went ashore 12 noon. Had a good feed and went sightseeing. Last time we were here it was dusk when we landed. Met a young chap last time I was here. He took me around in his car then back to his home for tea. His mother and father can only speak Spanish but his sister can speak English. Had a real good time with them. Left them about 8 o'clock and went to Apostleship of the Sea. Saw picture of Graf Spee.

CHAPTER 12

18th Apr to 11th May 1940

The Guns, They Make Me Deaf, You Know

Montevideo seems to have been a frequent port of call for Hawkins, now it was time to put into port again, but this time it was Buenos Aires, one hundred miles further west up the River Plate from Montevideo and Ronnie's fourth South American country in as many months.

It's not clear why Hawkins would go to B.A. when they had a good supply base at Monte. Argentina had quite a large German population and although neutral, along with the rest of South America at that time, the Argentine Government were less sympathetic to the British than Uruguay. Even after Pearl Harbour in 1942,

Argentina, along with Chile, were the only South American nations who refused to sever relations with the Axis powers and only declared war on Germany and Japan in 1944 when it was clear who the winning side would be. A gesture to pacify the USA no doubt but the government led by Juan Peron were happy to allow fugitive Nazi's a safe haven.

This lean towards the Axis didn't stop the Argentines from trading with Britain. Before the First World War Argentina was one of the fastest growing economies in the world until a succession of dictatorships dragged down prosperity and development. Massive herds of beef still roamed the pampas no matter who ran the country and during the war Argentina was an important supplier of cattle to Britain. So perhaps Hawkins coming to town was a reassurance to the Argentine-British and a reminder to the Government that Britannia still ruled the waves.

However, politics were not as important as having enough money in your pocket to buy a pint. According to Ron, a spot of shore leave could cost a month's wages. No surprise then that the lads took advantage of the hospitality of the British locals. The Empire was on the wane in 1940, but the legacy of immigrants drawn to Argentina (and Uruguay) because of strong trade links, had left a social set only too glad to entertain 'our boys' and Ronnie was not one to turn his generous nose up at a party.

Perhaps having a drink was a medicinal attempt to blot out Ronnie's ear ache. When I was a kid he was always shouting at me to "speak up". Admittedly I was quietly spoken as a lad but I always put his deafness down to the fact that he was 'old'. I never knew that it was a war wound caused by being too close to the 7.5" gun when it was fired.

It's hard to imagine what that must have been like, but the Hawkins main armament used sixty-two pounds of cordite to fire a two hundred pound shell a distance of nineteen kilometres. Being anywhere near that when it went off must have been dangerous in the extreme. They had the flash gear (eventually) but ear defenders would have been good too. "I said, ear defenders..., oh never mind."

18TH APRIL. SINCE LEAVING MONTE WE'VE RUN INTO SOME FILTHY WEATHER

18th April. Since leaving Monte we've run into some filthy weather. All hands and below decks everything secured and it was rough. We nearly had our boats stove in. Met Queen of Bermuda.

19th April Fri. Going into Buenos Aries Monday (perhaps). Organised parties for shore leave. I don't think I'll enjoy myself, you see I'm broke. Monte just bust me and we didn't expect to touch port before pay day.

Risking a Soaking

Stopped Norwegian boat and boarded her. She had no cargo and she had no port to go to. Gave her the British signal code.

Sat 20 April. Weather nippy No.3 piped to be worn. Buzz going round we expect to be home in June, wish it was true, it's so damn monotonous this commission. We've done over 30,000 miles since we sailed, which is the length of six times a cruiser does in a two and a half years commission. And when we get into port it costs a months pay nearly to enjoy ones self, everything is fairly dear. We are right in the traffic lanes, meeting plenty of ships.

Sunday 28 April. Since I wrote in this book last, we've been into Buenos Aries. We had a great time. Better than I expected. Organised parties. Went to British Sports club and dance at night time. Went to church. Met a nice little girl. Florence Hinks. No beauty but sensible.

Buenos Aries Harbour

Mon 29 April. Contacted HMS Cumberland. Stayed with us and did manoeuvres with

us. *Ships just come out from England.
Stil painted home fleet colour. Buzz
going round she's to relieve us, think
we'll be going home shortly.*

*Tues 30th. Scheduled to do 7.5 and 4
inch shoot. Postponed on account of heavy
ground swell. Did Inclination exercises.
I hope Italy keeps her nose clean. If she
doesn't we'll be out here indefinitely.*

*Wed 1 May. Still carrying out
exercises up to 12 noon. Transfer some
mail for home. Cumberland left us at
12:00. Expect to pick her up again
shortly. To-date 30,450 miles in 109 sea
days, 121 day out.*

*Thurs 2 May. Oiled at sea over the
bow. Cumberland hove in sight while we
were doing it and anchored close to us.
Meanwhile the Captain Commander and other
officers came aboard to visit the
Admiral. Our skipper Cpt. Rotheram has
been ill and the buzz is he is leaving us
for a short time to recuperate, so is the
R.N.R Leiut Commander. His job is
identifying merchant ships. The oiler
Arndale went alongside Cumberland and
oiled her.*

Fri 3 May. We were supposed to do a shoot today but weather conditions forced us to cancel it. When the shoot does come off it will be a throw off shoot against the Cumberland and visa versa. I'm hash recorder.

Sat 4 May. Weather very chilly, of course it's winter down here now. Wonder if Alan been called up yet. Since Jan 9 when we did a full calibre 7.5 shoot I've had trouble with my ears. First they started running, now they have stopped running but they are very painful, am slightly deaf. You see the 4 inch is right above the 7.5 and I was practically standing alongside the muzzle when she fired. If they are no better when we reach England I think I'm slated for hospital.

Hawkins Main Armament Firing

Sun 5 May. Rio Grande on our star beam. Heading south. German ship still in harbour.

Mon 6 May. Usual routine, weather chilly. Contact oiler Alcantara wednesday to take skipper. It's lovely keeping a middle watch. Wet through and cold. I'll be glad when this lot's finished. It's monotonous stuck out here. I think 50% of the ships company would willingly swop places with a North Sea patrol. I'm due for hospital when we get back.

Wed 8th May. Sighted Alcantara at dawn. Anchored and lowered Pinnacle. Four Ratings transferred, one insane. Two hands board us, stores and provs taken aboard. Mostly Liverpool lads on board A.M.C Tanker sighted. Skipper leaves us. Commander takes over. Oil and take in more stores from tanker. 15 bags of mail for Alcantara, only parcel mail for us. Things certainly do look bad in Norway.

Thur 9th May. Paint ship. Due in Montevideo Sat morn

Fri 10 May. Germany done it again in Belgium, Holland and Luxembourg. I did think he'd keep out for a while longer. We were due to sail for home next month and now we might have to go to Dutch East Indies to look after the crews of Jerry ships interned there. We have taken aboard sufficient field uniforms (Kaki) to fit out half the ships company. Sighted ships (British) patrolling outside The Rio Grande. Plenty of seals about.

Sat 11th May. Heading for Rio Grande De Sol. We'll get that Jerry ship yet. Fog. Complete silence on the upper deck. Jerry might try and slip out. We picked up mail this morn. No Mirrors, subscription must have run out.

BA Footnote:-

While Ronnie was enjoying a pint and chatting up church girls in sunny South America, the Nazi's were running rampant in Europe. Its easy for us to look back from a Nazi free future and feel perhaps a little smug at having 'won the war', but in mid 1940 the unstoppable advance of Germany must have been a frightening prospect. Even an ordinary guy like Ronnie with his feet on an armour plated deck and a twelve-pounder gun by his side was wondering where it would all end. But for now there were plenty of seals to look at.

CHAPTER 13

12th May to 7th June 1940

Pickle Jars and Spies

Ronnie's desire to 'smack the Boche' remained unfulfilled but they still had to practice. A little sibling rivalry between the Navy and Marines obviously added some spice to gunnery practice. The 4" gun that Ronnie was assigned to was designed to be used as an anti-aircraft gun and could hurl a twelve pound projectile almost as high as Mount Everest at the rate of sixteen rounds per minute or a shot roughly every four seconds, which must have raised a sweat under all that anti-flash gear. There is no record of Ronnie firing at aircraft in anger but they did use the 4" gun to put a shot across the bows of a reluctant merchantman on occasion.

The presence of Hawkins in Montevideo was enough to put a shot across the bows of an Axis 5th Column coup attempt in early June. A heavy cruiser had massive firepower as well as a crew of around 800, including a company of Marines. All in all they would have represented a considerable force that could have been deployed against potential anti-government forces. Added reinforcements from the Americans no doubt represented enough of a deterrent to dissuade a Uruguayan take over by the enemy.

SUN 12 MAY. CLEARED LOWER DECK. THE JIMMY SPOUTED ABOUT DISCIPLINE

Sun 12 May. Cleared lower deck. The Jimmy spouted about discipline etc & how he's going to run the ship. We take it good naturedly. Altered course for Falklands 8 o'clock this morning.

Monday. Weather growing colder. Fine with flat calm. 4" shoot tomorrow. Hope we do alright and beat the Marines, who have the two after guns.

Tue 14th May. We did 4" gun shoot this morning, 40 rounds. We didn't go @ all smoothly most of the lads were gun shy & were nervous. Still we got em all out an the burst were nicely placed. We beat the Marines. Every Officer & Petty Officer who had anything to do with the shoot were sure of that. The Admiral was pleased with us and commented on the excellent loading & laying. I'm a loader. Considering it's the first real shoot we've had we're alright. We are to have a regular monthly shoot. Weather still clear, sea getting a swell on. Cold.

4 inch Gun Crew

Wed 15 May. Sighted Falklands 08:30. Anchored 10:30. Oiler came alongside immediately & oiled us. She was also loaded with stores for us. Orders came through we had to sail Thurs forenoon. We had stores to get from store ships Baltaru & Ohiomel. We worked without a break except for meals till 11:30 & turned in.

Thur 16 May. Sailed 10-0 p.m. Weather misty, seas mountainous, course due south 25 knots. Wonder if we are chasing anything. Won if will round the Horn.

Sat 18 May. After steaming south for 30 hours we turned & headed north. Seas were worst I've seen yet we nearly turned turtle when we slewed. We were supposed to go to Dutch East Indies but received orders to return to Plate area as there are several large Italian ships there & relations with Italy are grave. Graver than the folks at home realise. We have all her ships under observance.

May 22. Heard our sister ship's gone down. Effingham. Electric storm for nearly a week. Oil tonight. Patrolling off Rio Grande de Sol. Effingham was our relief. She was to provision and oil etc and make her way out here. Looks like will be out here longer now.

Thur 23 May. Met tanker Arndale. Oiled. Weather breaking even. I'll be glad when we can get ashore & buy some cups. We are drinking out of jam jars, pickle jars, sugar and butter basins, jugs and tumblers and even milk tins.

June 1st 1940. I'm not keeping this diary daily as it's a waste of time. We've had an issue of cups and buried the pickle jars with due ceremony. 40 days at sea since we left B.A. Due in Monte Monday no shore leave. Situation in Belgium and Northern France seems to *favour us although retreating Italian situation very grave.*

June 4. Montevideo for stores. No individual shore leave. Jerry and Italian residents very truculent. Went to private grounds outside city and had bean feast. Big steak, mutton, sausage, greens and fruit & of course beer. At first they had no mineral waters but later they sent for some. Natives all for us. Cowboys & herders lent us their pony's. Great time. 10 letters from home. When we tied up we found that there was no mail. Later in the day a British mail boat arrived with 20 bags of mail aboard for us. Found out we were supposed to have foundered day after we left B.A. In the great storm which was raging. We also drove thru the city in buses.

June 7th Fri. Just found out why we went into Monte. Although we got stores aboard, we didn't take sufficient and we didn't oil. The reason is this. The government discovered a plot by the 5th column German & Italian's to take Montevideo in 2 hrs & the whole of Uruguay in 24. The fact that we were there prevented this and the rebels were all arrested. That's the reason there was no individual shore leave. 2 Yankee ships followed us and they're still there. The Marines were ready and I was in a landing party. We thought it was just drill in case we had to go home and were peeved when we found out what we missed. We met the oiler Olynthus two days after we left Monte & took a new Flag Lieutenant aboard. The situation in Monte is still grave. We still hope for action. The monotony of this job is driving me crazy.

CHAPTER 14

9th Jun to 6th Sep 1940

I'll fight till I die

The German blitzkrieg had pushed the British Expeditionary Force into the Channel at Dunkirk, France had fallen (much to Ron's disgust) and Italy had entered the war on the German's side. It was all looking pretty bleak, and Ron was feeling helpless on the other side of the world.

We know now how it all ended but in the summer of 1940 the possibility of Ronnie coming home to a Nazi flag flying over the Liver Buildings was distinctly on the cards. Ron must have been turning this scenario over in his head, contemplating how his mother might be able to survive if he and his brother Alan were lost. He's even weighing up who, between him and Alan, would be the best one for his Mother to 'lose'. But more worrying than the German take over of Europe and potential invasion of Britain was that there was only two weeks rum ration left!

Nine months into his tour of duty the novelty was wearing off big time. Ronnie wasn't anywhere near a proper fight with the enemy and his war had sunk into a routine that didn't match the glamour of the recruitment posters. Even Hawkins' supply ship the Alcantara had some action with the German Raider Thor.

Armed Merchant Raiders were a rather sneaky but very effective German weapon against Allied shipping. The Nazi strategy was to not confront the Royal Navy openly. Arms limitations following the First World War meant that the Germans concentrated less on building large conspicuous battleships but more on U-Boats and the small but powerful pocket battleships. Their idea was not to fight large scale naval battles but to concentrate on disrupting merchant shipping. The armed raider was perfect in this respect.

Fast merchant ships were armed with 5.9 or 6" guns which they camouflaged, then posed as merchant ships, commonly from neutral countries, to get close to their prey. They also carried canvas and timber to make false funnels, masts and other mock changes to their superstructures. The crew also had changes of uniform to make them look realistic. Hawkins was continually on the look out for these raiders as they sank and captured many ships over the course of the war.

HMS Cumberland, one of the other ships on South Atlantic patrol had gone back to Liverpool, Admiral Harwood was also leaving but there was no sign of Hawkins returning home. The realisation that they were out there for the duration was spelled out by the Admiral but like their diet of hard tack and bully beef it must have been a fact of life that was hard to swallow.

JUNE 9TH SUN. SPEEDED UP TO 24 KNOTS TO CATCH JERRY

June 9th Sun. Speeded up to 24 knots to catch Jerry ship this morning. She had slipped out of the Rio Grande & hugged the coast, putting into Monte & then out again and back to Rio. We'll get her yet.

14 June Fri. Italy entering the war has certainly altered things. We forced em into it. The Jerry's seem to be getting all their own way in France. It makes us feel miserable & we are all longing to go to the Med or North Sea. I hope France doesn't give up. I for one couldn't live under the Nazi regime. Not that they'll capture, but the struggle would be long and bitter and the folks at home would suffer. I wonder how Alan's got on. 8 weeks @ sea & two in harbour & 5 hours shore leave out of that. Can you wonder why we are going crackers here. I'm itching to get back & if possible I'm joining a naval battalion or the Army.

June 16 Sun. Germany is still pushing the French back. If they can only hold on until we get our men trained & armed we'll win. If the French give in God help us. We oiled today @ sea & took` aboard stores off the Arndale. I can't imagine Britain subject to the Nazi's.

June 17 Mon. We heard today that France had capitulated & believe me my heart turned over. I can't imagine England being subjugated. The feeling on this ship is one of frustration, stuck out here immobile. I hope Britain sticks out till the end. I'll fight till I die. As for France I thought they had more guts.

June 18 Tues. Today is rather a red letter day for me. I signed off the sick bay after 5 months attendance. I have had bad ears, discharging all the while & unbelievably painful. I told the doctor that the treatment he was giving me was tormenting my ears & asked him if he could give me olive oil treatment. Instead he gave me glycerine and my ears steadily improved. The Admiral gave us a speech and asked us to keep our spirits up & to drill & become if possible more efficient. We'll fight to the bitter end. My only hope is that Mother isn't left destitute. I'd sooner go under than Alan, he's a tradesman & can earn even under another rule.

June 20. Due to meet AMC Altcantara & drop mail, receive mail & stores. Situation in Montevideo very grave, Yankee cruisers & Argentine gunboats in vicinity, we are standing by & we have been told to hold ourselves ready for landing parties. German's trying to take control there & a corps of motorcycle troops (Jerry) 500 strong are trying to terrorise the people. Just had news that the day we chased the Wakama another Jerry the Wolfsburg sighted us & thinking we were after her scuttled herself.

June 22 Sunday. Took mail aboard from British trawler which is proceeding to Falklands. Landing party formed. I'm one of em. I hope we do land & have a smack @ the Boche. Nothing would please me better.

30 June Sunday. We put into Rio & were there 36 hours. There are about 5 Italian ships there. I think the Pretoria Castle has taken over our patrol for a

short while & we are staying up here.
It's very warm. We are in tropical rig.

Hot Weather (Ron on left)

July 1st Mon. Since we left the oiler
we have been patrolling the islands and
bays which abound on the coast for a
submarine berth.

July 4th Fri. To date we have been at
sea 182 days and out of that 12 days in
harbour. We've steamed 48,357 miles.

8th July Mon. We met *Pretoria Castle* & received orders to go back to our old station (Monte). We are back in the land or sea of mists & the weather is cold. We met *Arndale* & perhaps *Alcantara*. Capt. Oram of *Theitis* fame is taking over as new skipper & we are having 3 more firsts and a paymaster cadet. There is a lot of chopping & changing, chaps leaving going home & fresh chaps taking over. We've already had a new Flag Lieutenant. The Admiral is going home the end of this month. We were supposed to take him. We are always getting our orders changed. Pity the Admiralty can't busy em selves with the home ship. Leave these out here to the man on the spot Admiral Harwood. I'm two blocks.

July 10 Wed. We've been two days now trying to oil & transfer Oram & Snots from *Alcantara*. The weather has been too "ruff" & we are hanging around here. We're south of River Plate and it's damned cold. There is a faint hope of our being returned. The *Cornwall* is due out here end of this month. She "mite" be taking our place.

12 July Fri. Orange Day. Plenty of good natured chuff. We've been anchored *all day since the seas have subsided. Fog came down @ dawn & the other two ships have been unable to find us.*

19 July Fri. Today is the first fine day we've had for over a week & that is because we are heading north. We managed to pick the skipper up. He came aboard @ midnight & believe me the seas were ruff. 4 Snotties & 4 Stokes came aboard next morning & we oiled & stored ships. We were in Monte for 24 hrs to pick up mail & provs.

Sunday 21st July. Heading north. Warmer. Cpt. Oram tightening up. Discontent in ship. I used to work, now I loaf. They should send us home and let one of the cruisers who've been in Arctic take our place.

Captain Oram - HMS Hawkins

Tues 23rd July. Put into secluded bay to oil. Armed raider in the vicinity. Hope we meet her. Finished oiling in record time. Routine shot to hell. The skipper says the ship is dirty below decks. More scrubbing chipping painting than that. Says he likes to see his men in comfortable clean quarters. When we finish below decks start on upper deck. I don't do much as I'm side party.

Wed 24th July. Bit of a thrill today. Alarm sounded & we rushed to our action stations.

Action Station 4 Inch Gun

We were all closed up in less than 5 minutes 5:30pm the time. We looked around after we manned the gun & saw a ship running full speed. We increased to 26 knots & overtook her. She wouldn't answer our signals so we (our gun) fired a shot across her bows making her heave to. False alarm tho' she was a Norwegian under British hands & she thought we were Italian ship.

July 28 Sun. Had a nasty toss this forenoon. Was standing @ the top of ladder when ship gave a lurch landed up on Marines mess-deck below. Not badly hurt wrenched my innards fit for duty. Volunteered for crash cutters crew and I've been picked. 06:50 great activity among the Gold Braid. Admiral and Skipper dashed to the chart room. 06:55 News just come thru' Alcantara engaged enemy raider & a hot fight is going on (See Pathé Newsreel https://youtu.be/aLj88hB4lkI). *Raider has 6 - 5.9" guns plus various small armament. Alcantara 9 - 6" the raiders guns outrange our 7.5" by 7,000 yards. We turned 180 degrees & set off towards em @ 25 knots. 17:00 raider turned tail & ran. Our ship has a shell in her engine room & is down to 10 knots. The enemy is 750 miles away & is heading towards us at 15 knots. We might meet her about dawn tomorrow. Just our blooming luck we were on that patrol 2 days ago.*

2 Aug Fri. We ran into a quiet bay yesterday and oiled. Crash cutters crew was called away. Commander pleased with show we made. Still looking for raider. Dashing around @ 20 knots since Monday. Vindictive reported on way out to relieve us. Sister ship to us. I'm sending St Anthony after the raider. Let's hope he'll find it. Cumberland reported in

Liverpool. She was due here with us a couple of months ago. Great calamity 14 day rum left in ship. All the lads worried stiff.

Sat 3 Aug. Today I doubt we've steamed 10 miles. We have been steaming 5 knots against a 4½ knot tide. Various ships we've talked with have reported a mystery ship in this vicinity & we are waiting for it.

Aug 4 Sun. 6 knots our speed we are waiting bang in the centre of the trade routes waiting for the next S.O.S. and then we pounce. We do a shoot tomorrow. It's probable that the raider beats it to the Indian Ocean now that she's been detected. Falklands end of this month. Running short of provisions & Rum.

Aug 6 Tues. We did the A.A. Shoot yesterday. The sea was ruff and the target we launched for L.A. Shoot capsized. The crash cutters crew was sent out to retrieve it. The skipper is dead nuts on us his crew.

Aug 10. Oiled today. The cutter went away last night and again this morning. We collected the mail last night. Weather is bitter. We got stores and provs from the oiler. Not much but it'll have to last us. Since my last entry we've had a hell of a storm. 60 foot waves washing right over the bridge & I haven't been dry for 4 days.

Rough Weather

Aug 12 Mon. We've been on hard tack and Bully Beef alternate days. There are two raiders in the South Atlantic. Commodore Pegram is our Admirals relief. I shall be sorry to see him go.

Aug 20th Tues. This last two days we stored ship from Boltavia & oiled from Arndale. We needed both badly we've been at sea now for 5 weeks & we need a break, no news of raiders.

Sept 6. We are at Montevideo. The Alcantara is here as well. We picked up Com. Pegram a few days ago. At B.A a few days ago & we were supposed to come to Monte right away so as the Com. Could take over from Harry. Heavy seas prevented us & it was cold more than that. When we leave here we are going up to Rio & oil & then across to Simonstown for a few days & then round to Durban for a refit & then back here. We are out here for the duration. Capt. Oram doesn't keep us in the dark regarding movement of the ship and we keep quiet in port. Whereas when we only heard buzzes we didn't worry so much. The Enterprise is relieving us. I still have an idea we the AA guns crews will go home sooner than we expect. Maybe on the Yankee destroyers. The Admiral in his farewell speech said it's very difficult to tell you you'll be out here for the duration. Especially when I pass my friends on the AA gun every morning sheltering in the lee of the forrad funnel. I know how difficult and hard it is for you especially them to be out of it. Still it's in the lap of the God's and I'll do my best for you.

CHAPTER 15

14th Sep 1940 to 4th Jan 1941

Off to Africa

Ron knew that Italy entering the war would have big consequences for him and his ship. Sure enough, by the autumn of 1940, with the war hotting up in Africa, Hawkins was diverted away from shipping protection off the River Plate to convoy duty around Africa.

The Italian invasion of British Somaliland followed by their invasion of British held Egypt was becoming a threat to the Middle East oil fields that Churchill wasn't prepared to contemplate. Hitler had taken his eye off the British ball and was looking towards Russia. This meant that Churchill could take troops away from the home front and send them to defend North Africa. The

Mediterranean was too dangerous to risk large troop convoys so they were sent to the Red Sea ports and Aden via the Cape of Good Hope. These convoys had complete divisions of troops along with all their equipment and stores and were known as the Winston Specials.

This change of tack was a welcome diversion for Ronnie. HMS Hawkins was in need of a refit after a long patrol. Ronnie needed a refit too and South Africa was a chance to have his ears looked at in hospital. The treatment comprised mostly of hot baths, plenty of sleep and plenty to eat, which to Ronnie must have been just what the doctor ordered.

Before Ronnie could have his holiday though, Captain Oram must have thought he'd find some pugilistic action for Ronnie and some of the other Liverpudlians on board. Stopping off mid ocean at the very remote Gough Island, the Captain sent a rowing boat full of scousers watched over by the Padre and the First

Officer armed with just a pistol, to look for a German armed raider hiding out in a lonely inlet.

A few hundred German sailors against Ronnie and his mates must have seemed reasonable odds to the optimistic Oram. They didn't find the Raider but they didn't come back empty handed either, having picked up a penguin as compensation. You can take the lads out of Liverpool but you can't take Liverpool out of the lads!

SEPT 14 SAT. WE REALLY ARE ON OUR WAY TO AFRICA.

Sept 14 Sat. We really are on our way to Africa. On the way we are calling at Gough Island in the S. Atlantic 200 miles South of Tristan Da Cuna to see if the raiders are using it as a base. I hope I'm a landing party. Strong buzz the Mersey lads are on draft & that we'll be

*drafted to a frog destroyer @ Simonstown.
Then we are for the Med (perhaps).*

All Scousers

*18th Sept Wed. Yesterday morning (Tues)
we sighted Gough Island about 07:h00. We
cruised around it carefully thru'
glasses. Crash Cutters crew was piped &
when we got up there a whalers crew was
picked, myself included & away we went.
Included with there was a Snotty, L.
Commander, Padre from Tristan Da Cunha
who is taking passage on us, a bunting*

tosser & a spare man. 10 men in all. Only the Jimmy was armed as there was no sign of the island being occupied. Still, as the Commander said, "I've picked you lads because you can use your fists." We had a good pull & as we drew near the shore we ran in a mass of seaweed or kelp, as the natives of this part of the world call it. It took a while to get thru. We managed finally and as we drew near the beach it was impossible to land on account of boulders. So we tied up to an outcrop and waded ashore. The island was uninhabited apart from penguins, seals and birds. We caught two penguins & took em aboard to show the lads. I've never been in a more desolate place than Gough Island.

Gough Island

Dec 14. It's been a long time since I opened the book so I give a brief summary of the events. On Sept 21st we docked @ Simonstown (Snooky) & much to my surprise I was shunted off to hospital on the assumption my ears were no good. I was there for nineteen days & had no treatment whatever. I had a real good time tho' out in cars every day. All night in bed. Lots of good hot baths and plenty of good grub. I put on over a stone while I was there & kept it on while I was ashore. On coming out of hospital I was attached to working party ashore Africander 1. I did nothing

*however but escort duty. Bringing
deserters back. A most distasteful job.
The ship was @ Durban refitting & the
lads were having 6 days leave. I applied
for leave, was refused. Applied to join
ship, refused. So I set out to have a
good time. Plenty of swimming, plenty of
climbing, plenty of girls. The girls are
a really decent crowd. Sent to Durban as
escort to two Aussies who'd deserted. Had
short stop at Kimberley, Bloemfontain,
Ladysmith, Bethlehem. 3 days on train
each way. Good time. Saw Hawkins there.
She'll be at Snooky in a weeks time. I've
tried my hardest to get drafted to
another ship but to no avail. Even
volunteered for S. Service but it was no
use. Sent on board Hawkins, given a
rousing welcome by the lads. I don't
think we are going to S America just yet.
We did a week shooting & then set off to
pick up a convoy. Met a crowd of
Liverpool boys on Hermes in Snooky. We
picked up a fast convoy, 20 knots, & took
em around to Durban. I was unable to get
ashore. Returned to Snooky for repairs to
degaussing gear. Met worst storm I've
ever seen. Ship damaged.*

Smashed up Boat

Over a week in Snooky. Xmas day at sea, not a bad time.

Christmas Concert

Dec 28 Fri. Going north to Freetown to pick up convoy. Hot. Forgot to mention Free French Sloop in Snooky. We took a fast trip to Freetown & arrived 30th Dec.

Xmas Concert

Dec 31. Went ashore. Scruffy place, it stinks. There must be over 150 ships in harbour. Big convoy for Liverpool wish we were taking em.

1 Jan New Year's Day. Hot. Shore rig tropical suits and topees. We've been out of England a year & it's over a year since I was home. I forgot to mention, the day I came aboard from hospital the ship cleared for action & sailed after a Vichy ship. 3 days searching failed to produce same.

2 Jan. Roused out of our hammocks 23:00 & cleared for sea. Sailed 01:00 destination unknown. Maybe we'll see some action.

4 Jan. Sighted lifeboat 08:35. 10 survivors from British Premier. Torpedoed 10 days ago. All men exhausted. Two detained in sick bay. Proceeding on job.

Survivors of SS British Premier

SS British Premiere Footnote:-

The SS British Premier was bringing oil from the Persian Gulf as part of a convoy bound for Swansea. Straggling behind the main convoy she was spotted by U-Boat U-65 and torpedoed 200 miles South West of Freetown, Sierra Leone. Thirty-two men were lost, Hawkins picked up nine men after being adrift for ten days.

HMS Faulknor picked up four more men after being adrift for 41 days, of which 25 days were without food. The men had initially dived overboard but after three hours in the water were able to get back on board and release a lifeboat. They lost their water in the process and were only saved from death when it rained several days later.

U-65 was the first U-Boat to cross the equator and was responsible for sinking twelve ships and damaging another three before finally being sunk by the Destroyer HMS Douglas with the loss of all her 50 crew.

CHAPTER 16
12th Jan to 28th Sep 1941

The Winston Special Convoys and Italian Prizes
As Ronnie moved into the second year of the war, it's becoming clear that hostilities are not going to end any time soon and that he's not about to get home in the foreseeable future.

His diary entries become shorter, less descriptive and sometimes terse. He's concentrating on the movements of the ship and it's encounters. There is less personal reflection and anecdotes about ship life, he's become 'non-battle' hardened. We only get glimpses of what's going on inside his head and it's not good. Phrases like "Eagle and Nelson leave, good riddance," and "went ashore, scruffy place, it stinks", (of Freetown), betray a growing dissatisfaction with his lot.

It could be that convoy duty and chasing raiders (and not finding them) meant a lot of time closed-up around the gun. The cocktail of tension and tedium would exact a mental toll on the crews, Ronnie included.

The weather was either incredibly hot or stormy, as some of Ronnie's photos testify, neither of which was good news in their exposed position on deck.

Britain and especially Liverpool were being blitzed. Ron's Mum and sisters lived in Bath Street that ran along the side of the docks. I'm not sure how much Ronnie would have known about the danger his family were in but it must have been a worry.

Supplies for the war effort poured through the Liverpool docks and it regularly rained bombs around Ma

Turner's (my elder brother and sister grew up playing on the bomb sites that surrounded the house.)

Ronnie had also damaged his ears that were probably painful. As a kid I knew Ronnie was prone to being grumpy and shouty on occasion. I put it down to his 'Turner' temperament, a fiery streak of unpredictability that ran through the family. But it could also have been depression that had its root in his war experiences. It wasn't a condition that drew much attention in those days.

The happy times of parties thrown by South American British communities were behind him now, but there were still highlights, such as swimming in the warm waters of Mombasa and being given free reign to clobber drunken Frenchmen on prize ships. Being promoted to Leading Seaman wasn't bad either.

For the ship, 1941 was a seminal year. Hawkins played a major part in safely shepherding the troops to North

Africa where Britain would inflict its first major victories over both the Italians and Germans and ultimately retake North Africa in preparation for the invasion of Italy. She played a significant part in retaking British Somaliland from the Italians and captured a number of Italian ships. All big stuff and Ronnie was a part of all that and I'm proud that he was.

Sun 12. We are now 3 days out from Freetown.

Sun 12. We are now 3 days out from Freetown. We start off with convoy of 18 slow ships. Escort by us, Dorsetshire, Norfolk, aircraft carrier Formidable, 2 destroyers, 2 sloops & AMC. 2 day out Formidable & two cruisers left us to go in search of Raider.

Devonshire joined us. Destroyer sank a U-Boat. I hope it's the one which sank B. Premier. Destroyers have turned back & we continue with 7 knot convoy to Durban. Expect to get there 25 of this month. Am trying to pass for Killick (Leading Seaman).

Sat 25 Jan. Recalled from convoy on 21st & ordered to Cape Town in a rush. We are to escort Formidable somewhere. Spent Thur & Fri nights in Capetown & sailed for Snooky. Sat morn arr.12:30. Ammunitioned. Something in the wind. We might go into the med.

Thur 30th Sailed with Formidable Sat night. Proceeding to Aden. Think she's taking Illustrious place. I hope we take Southhampton's place. We put into Mombasa for oil Sat morn.

Aircraft Carrier HMS Formidable

Sat 1st Feb. Arr Mombasa 08:00 left 14:00.

Sun 2 Feb. The Captain cleared lower deck today & told us that originally the Formidable's planes were to bomb 2 places in Italian Somaliland & we were to go in and bombard at the same time. When we left Mombasa orders reached us to proceed to a position 700 miles east where a ship had been attacked and sunk by a raider. We proceeded for a few hours & were then recalled & told to continue on our voyage to Aden. The bombing and bombardment being washed out as we had passed our objective the skipper of the Formidable had decided to carry out the bombing of one place off his own bat. @ 17:00 tonight 14 planes took off & proceeded towards land. To date we are waiting for their return. 20:00 planes returning. 21:00 all planes safely returned. Operation a success.

5 Feb. Aden Moored 08:00. 6 Feb. Sailed 1200. 9 Feb Arrived Mombasa. 10 Feb left Mombasa with HMS Hermes. Bombardment coming off soon. With Shropshire, Capetown Ceres.

11 Feb. Tues. Overhauled Italian ship. Placed prize crew aboard. SS Adria. 2 hours later captured SS Savoia. Placed prize crew aboard. Casualties 1 Italian wounded badly. He's onboard now. The prize crew onboard Adria captured another.

SS Adria - Italian Prize – With Aircraft from Hermes

SS Savoia Italian Prize

12 Feb. Captured two more Italian ships & 1 German. German scuttled by her skipper. Our lads went aboard and shut watertight doors. Hope she'll float. Wounded Italian died and buried over the side.

13 Feb. Went back to German ship the Ukermark. Still afloat though low in water.

Ukkermark Settling After Scuttling

German Prisoners from the Ukkermark

14 Feb. Bombardment tomorrow. Kisamayu our objective Ceres To take her in tow if poss.

15 Feb. Ceres took Ukermark in tow but she sank. Went in to bombard Kisamenyu but found place deserted. Our troops have taken over. Went further up the coast to bombard ? Mogadisiu but cancelled @ last minute. Contacted Shropshire. Submarine spotted. Left her to a destroyer although we closed up @ action stations. Felt slight shudder.

16 Feb. Just cruising around.

20 Enroute for Mombasa. Expect to oil & catch up convoy.

21st Mombasa. Divers sent down to examine our screw. Damaged. Must have hit Sub a glancing blow.

22nd. Lovely Swimming here. We were in the water for 4 hours at a time.

Bingo

Whist

23. *Sailed for convoy. S.O.S. from ship attacked by raider 150 mile away contacted Glasgow by wireless. Raider German battle cruiser. Cleared for action, Glasgow on other side of her &*

closing in. Scrap doesn't come off Glasgow told to shadow her.

24 Contact convoy. HMS Australia gives us mail. 72 bags. 1 letter & 2 Xmas cards for me very poor. Australia goes to join Glasgow, Shropshire, Emerald, Capetown, Ceres, Hermes & 1 or 2 others closing around raider. I hope they get her. I reckon we've been done in the eye being done out of four scraps.

Sun 26. Still with convoy bound for Aden. Crossed the line 14 times. Gross tonnage of convoy almost 500,000 tons.

Middle East Convoy Escort

1 Sun March. Left convoy last night in Red Sea 12 hours steaming from Port Sudan. Bound for Aden in a hurry. We touched Aden with Duchess of Richmond oiled & returned to convoy.

15 March. My birthday. We took convoy half way up Red Sea then returned to Aden. Started patrol of island north of Madagascar looking for signs of raider. Visited Seychelles, Faquer, Agalega, Algebra, Assumption etc. No sign, cruising round. Passed out Killicks exam don't know how I got on.

17 March. St Patricks day. Went ashore Seychelles Port Victoria, Mahea Island. 93 islands in this group. Language French. People Shakies ie. All races mixed. French predominating, not a bad place. Good swimming, plenty of sharks & women - no good.

March 18. Saw Commander. Passed Killicks exam. Papers have to go to England. While searching islands received word Von Scheer was anchored off Alebra proceeded full speed, found the news was a month old. Heavy air raids in Liverpool. Worried stiff.

March 27. Arr. Mombasa. March 28 Still here. Leave this evening. Leave 16:00. Left.

March 30. Contacted convoy Glasgow & Illustrious. We take Glasgow's place. No planes on Illustrious.

March 31. Italian prisoner died, buried overside.

April 1st bound for Durban. 7 days self refit 48 hours leave each watch. Crossed line 18th time. Arrived Durban 4th April order to proceed to sea immediately. All leave cancelled. Orders cancelled. Sailed Simonstown 14 April arrived 18th. Touched East London on way down. Left 20th with ½ convoy north 10 ships in convoy 25,000 troops. Picked up other part of convoy ½ million tons of shipping & 60,000 troops.

28 April left convoy to Glasgow & Colombo. Bound for Mombasa. Be glad of a few days rest.

29 April. Arrived Mombasa 09:00 left 16:00. Escorting Eagle aircraft carrier. 5th one we've escorted. Destination?

29 April. Chasing raider. Hope we get it.

May 5th Raider cornered in .neutral port in Madagascar. Vichy government. 72 hours respite. We'll get her when she comes out.

May 6th. Cornwall joined us. Of all the damned luck. We are to sweep with Eagle & see if we can find Raiders supply ship. Leave raider. I'm disgusted.

May 9th. Arrived Durban. Have been detailed as Leadsman. **Raider sunk by Cornwall.** *Nelson in dock.*

May 10th. Eagle & Nelson leave, good riddance.

May 31st. Since my last entry we have left Durban. Picked up a convoy off Cape Good Hope & the dirtiest weather I've seen. 4 boats smashed. Guard on Vichy 6,000 tons, 1,700 Indo Chinese troops aboard, crew drunk. Soon settled em. Left Durban today for the north with convoy.

June 22nd. Picked for prize crew. Left convoy Aden since then been to Seychelles & patrolling. Bound for ......

Sept 28. We are going home soon for a refit. Thank God.

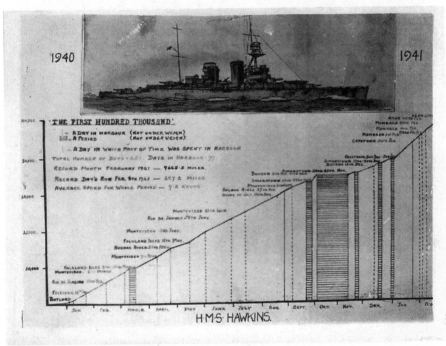

HMS Hawkins Distance Log

CHAPTER 17

We are going home - thank God

"We are going home soon for a refit. Thank God."

That one line seems to sum up everything that Ron felt about his situation at the end of 1941. Reading between the lines, I think he was very much at the end of his tether. Hawkins was back in the UK for a much-needed refit in November 1941 and Ronnie never went back on board. His record shows he finished the war stationed at shore bases in North Africa and Italy. Why he didn't go back to sea I can only speculate. Perhaps his ears were playing up, maybe he was depressed or perhaps it was the whim of the Navy. He's not here now to ask.

After the war Ronnie returned to civvy life. The skills he learned manning an anti aircraft gun can hardly have been useful in peacetime Liverpool, but his time spent on long, uneventful watches was not entirely wasted. Ronnie could roll a cigarette with one hand and hide a lit fag in his mouth!

Ron became a foreman at the Bear Brand stocking and tights factory in Woolton, Liverpool, until retirement. He never married and lived at home with his brother Alan and sisters Rose and Edith in Wavertree and died of bowel cancer in 1988 aged 73.

The war plucked ordinary guys like Ronnie from mundane jobs and threw them into the front line. If they survived they were dumped back into mundanity. For many like Ronnie the war was the most exciting thing that happened in their whole lives. But the legacy of that 'excitement' was a heavy burden at times.

I'm lucky that my legacy is this wonderful insight into what the war was like for one of my family who did his bit for King and country. Ronnie never did get to have a full-on 'smack at the Boche', he made up for it by having a smack at anyone who wound him up, including an unlucky burglar who made the mistake of breaking into Ronnie's place one time. Even in his seventies he still gave the bloke a pasting. I'm glad he didn't end up at the bottom of the ocean or on a lonely Falklands hillside. I'm glad he came back and I'm glad he left his diary and photographs to share with all the generations to come.

Ronnie Turner in retirement

Please Consider Leaving A Review

Reviews are a massive help to other readers (and authors!)

books2read.com/Asmackat

You May Also Like To Join My Reader List

Join my reader list to get advanced notifications of new books and exclusive reader offers.

johnnyparker.uk/reader-list/

About the Author

Johnny Parker lives in Birkenhead, England, with his wife Andrea, two springer spaniels and two cats. Unlike his Uncle Ron, Johnny has never managed a 'smack at the Boche' but has demolished the odd German beer and sausage.

It's thanks to Ronnie and his generation that we are not all sausage eaters.

His writing credits include two kids' picture books that help to entertain a growing army of grandchildren, a professionally produced play 'Sting Like a Butterfly' and numerous prize-winning short stories.

For more information about Johnny and his writing go to johnnyparker.uk

Made in the USA
Columbia, SC
26 June 2017